Birthright?

Birthright?

Travelogue of an American Radical in Israel / Palestine

Nani Ferreira-Mathews

On Our Own Authority! Publishing.
Atlanta, Georgia

Birthright? –
Travelogue of an American Radical in Israel/Palestine

On Our Own Authority! Publishing.
Atlanta, Georgia.

ISBN-13: 978-0-9906418-7-2
ISBN-10: 0-9906418-7-2
LCCN: 2017906912

www.oooabooks.org
oooabooks@gmail.com

Cover art by Julia Simoniello

CONTENTS

1. A Diner in New York City 9

2. Newark International Airport 16

3. Haifa and Speed Dating 28

4. The Mikvah 39

5. Shabbat on the Kibbutz 46

6. Golan Heights and the Jordan River 60

7. Mifgash Begins, Tel Aviv 74

8. Exhaustion at Masada and the Dead Sea 83

9. A Night at a Bedouin "Camp" 93

10. Silence From Gaza to the West Bank 98

11. Yad Vashem and Holocaust Guilt 106

12. The Western Wall and the End of Mifgash 121

13. Final Day: Did someone say "Birthrate"? 131

ACKNOWLEDGMENTS

I would like to thank Andrew Zonneveld for helping me in every step of this book's process. From conception to completion, your insight and dedication to this project has been priceless. The conversations we shared in the days I was in Israel/Palestine were eye opening for us both. Thank you for sharing this journey with me.

A special thanks to Lys Riganti, who helped me pack that bag the morning I left and who was a constant support to me while I was abroad and when I came home. Thank you for your encouragement as I wrote these chapters all the way to their end. Your feedback helped shape this work and made it stronger. I hope you enjoy reading it in its entirety, finally.

Thank you to Lelach Shani for putting me in touch with your loving family in Haifa and Tel Aviv and for sharing your childhood kibbutz experiences with me.

Thank you to my cousin Nicholas Mathews. The direction of my life was greatly affected by the whirlwind of talks we shared while I visited you and Makoto in Tokyo. Thank you for hosting me and for asking me "what's next?"

Thank you to Nir Melamed, my host in Tel Aviv, for answering any questions I had and for authentically sharing your life experience and home with me.

Thank you to my Aunt Lois and Uncle Barry in Los Angeles. Thank you for hosting me and answering my questions about our family history. Special thanks for sending me home with some great picture keepsakes of my grandparents and parents.

Thank you to my mom and dad, Wild Bill and Princess. The love you two have given me and the support I've received from you throughout my life is a debt I could never repay. Thank you for the video chats while I was away and for keeping me alive, both as a child and to this day. I love you both so much.

Finally, I would like to thank and dedicate this book to my Grandma Sandy. Your love and legacy has stretched far beyond your early departure from this world. The Jewish traditions you brought to our family inspired this entire work. I have a feeling that you would read these pages with hesitancy, but I know that you would understand that this work is not an attack on our faith, but instead, an honest examination of a deeply concerning form of nationalism.

Chapter 1: A Diner in New York City

"You're Jewish; don't fight it!" my good friend proclaimed behind a cup of coffee in a crowded Lower East Side diner, just a few years ago.

The conversation began with some harmless references to comedian David Cross. However, things really switched gears when we came to the topic of his stand-up routine about Judaism.

"Look, I'm not certain that David Cross has any authority in this," I replied.

Despite my lifelong irreverence and being fully convinced that I was not Jewish, the conversation, or debate, continued.

"It doesn't matter what you think. It's not about how you feel. It's a fact. You are Jewish," my dinner-mate said, matter-of-factly adjusting his glasses and leaning in over the table.

"I do not accept your facts, sir!" I said, smiling in rebuttal.

For those unaware of the David Cross skit in reference, it goes like this:

David Cross to Rabbi: "I don't believe in God so I can't be Jewish, right?"

David Cross imitating Rabbi's response: "Lemme ask you one question. You say this now but was your mother's vagina Jewish?"

David Cross: "Yes, yes it was. Fuck, yes. You got me on a technicality. So, no matter what I believe, Judaism is the only religion that won't allow you to not be Jewish."

I looked over the table after this law was announced and pleaded with my judge, "But I didn't come out of Jewish vagina; I came out of a Hawaiian vagina."

My mom's mother was full-blooded Hawaiian, my mother half, and myself one-fourth. If I ever identified as anything, it was as Hawaiian. It was my mom's stepmother who came from a Jewish background. My father was from Italian Catholic roots, which were quickly dismissed.

"No, it doesn't matter. Your grandma was Jewish; your mom did Jewish stuff, therefore, you are from a Jewish vagina," he declared loudly into the bustling diner.

I smirked as I gave into the peer pressure. After all, it didn't seem appropriate to publicly deny my Jewish heritage in one of the oldest Jewish neighborhoods in New York City.

I was not brought up in any type of religious household. My parents do not hold onto any religion and never had a mind to share any traditions with us. My mother's stepmother was my only link to Judaism. She brought her Jewish faith to my mother and her four siblings. Passover, Bar Mitzvahs, Hanukkah, etc. were all celebrated in my mother's youth. My mother told us stories, but she never shared practices. Still, according to my friend (and David Cross), I was Jewish. Apparently, there was no escaping it.

At first, I didn't think much of this decree. I was not close to my grandmother and she died when I was young. However, this short jest stuck in my mind.

We received Hanukkah gifts when I was young and my mother shared stories of my cousins Bar Mitzvahs. I had once asked why I never had a Bat Mitzvah and my mother only responded with, "You can if you want one."

Not really knowing what it meant, I didn't press any further. But now, I was wondering what it meant to Jewish. I had just become a New York City transplant a few months earlier and was exposed to a vast Jewish culture I had never witnessed in the southeastern United States. A mixture of curiosity and new surroundings implored me to explore further.

I called my mother a few days after this conversation.

"Mom, I'm Jewish," I explained to her, "or so I'm told."

"No you're not," she responded chuckling on the other end.

"Why are you laughing!?" I exclaimed. "I've accepted it now. I'm Jewish," I cried back at her.

"What makes you think this? You never did anything Jewish, except when you pretended to be Jewish in high school to ditch all the holidays," she delivered back to me.

It was true that I knew my mother was sort-of Jewish, so I used that as an excuse to miss a lot of days in my senior year of high school. Being raised in the Bible Belt of rural Georgia, no one of authority knew any of the holidays anyway. I only knew them from a calendar that I kept in my room, and I stayed to task that year, taking every Jewish holiday off, high and low. I may have accidentally taken Ramadan off as well. Still, no one noticed.

I explained the rules of Jewish identity as I learned them from my friend a few nights before.

"My vagina isn't Jewish!" she exclaimed, laughing.

I was happy to amuse her. In fact, I was quite amused by the whole situation myself.

After we spoke, I began asking more questions about Jewish holidays to my Jewish friends. Most of them found it amusing that I was taking such a late interest in the faith.

The summer after that first conversation in the diner, I met a young woman in a beer garden who had just gotten back from Birthright.

"You've never heard of Birthright?!" she exclaimed.

"No," I answered flatly.

"Oh, and you said you were Jewish right?" she asked.

"Yeah, my grandmother was," I answered honestly.

"Okay, so you have to go on Birthright. It's a trip to Israel and it's completely free." She paused to take a drag from her cigarette.

"If you are Jewish and under twenty-six years old." She added.

"Wait, What?" I asked in complete shock.

"Yep. It's a ten-day trip paid for by Israel and a bunch of donations from philanthropic Jews who love Israel."

"Go on," I replied.

"Yeah, so if you're Jewish this organization that gets all these donations will pay for you to go to your homeland, or whatever," she said as she took another drag.

"Hmm," was all I could reply.

I had just returned from a long backpacking trip and I wasn't interested in traveling, so I didn't look into it for some time. It was almost a year later when I consulted the Internet to research this mysterious free trip I heard about from a stranger the past summer. I clicked on the first website I saw and scrolled to the FAQs:

1. What is Birthright?

Taglit-Birthright Israel is a unique, historical partnership between the people of Israel through their government, local Jewish communities [...] and leading Jewish philanthropists.

2. What does the gift cover?

The Taglit-Birthright Israel gift covers round trip airfare (from designated cities), hotel accommodations, transportation, at least two meals per day and other associated land costs (such as admission to sites) for ten-day trips to Israel offered by approved Trip Organizers.

A button on the banner below read, "Summer Registration Now Open."

I called my mother after I registered.

"Remember how we are Jewish?" I asked immediately without saying hello.

"Yes Nani, I remember you think you are Jewish because my of vagina or something," she answered.

"Whatever Mom. You are Jewish, your mom was Jewish, we are Jewish, and I'm going to Israel because it's free." I said with conviction.

"Wait, what? If you're Jewish they just pay for you to go to Israel? What's the catch?"

* * *

"Hello," I answered the phone softly.

I was expecting the qualifying interview for the Birthright trip.

"Hello, I'm calling for Nani" answered a happy voice over the phone.

"Yes, this is she," I replied, knowing this was the call I had been anticipating.

"This is Sara and I'm calling from Birthright!" she exclaimed with immeasurable excitement.

"Yes," I replied again, flatly.

She had such high energy it could make a cheerleader wince.

"I just need to ask you a few questions and get you ready for your free trip to Israel!" she replied into the phone.

"Great!" I replied semi-mockingly. She didn't seem to notice.

"Are your parents Jewish?" she asked.

"My mother is. My father is not." I replied curtly.

"Great!" she exclaimed. Apparently I was answering correctly.

She continued, "What holidays did you celebrate growing up?"

This was a bit trickier to answer. I wasn't raised with any religion. I remembered getting an Easter basket or two when I was younger. We celebrated Christmas most years, until we all seemed to lose interest. I had celebrated Hanukkah with a friend when I was younger. I answered honestly.

"Easter. Hanukkah, sometimes. Christmas here and there. We weren't really religious," I responded, hoping this was also the right answer.

"Okay. Great!" she exclaimed. I seemed to be passing her test.

"Do you consider yourself Jewish?" she asked.

I thought back on the conversation with my mother and my friend and answered honestly,

"Yes. I'm Jewish."

"Great! I only have a few more questions."

She fired off a few other questions about the lineage on my mother's side. We never spoke of my father's heritage.

"Great!" she exclaimed again. "Nani, do you have any dietary restrictions we should know about for the flight?" she asked in summation.

"No," I responded carefully, hoping I wasn't expected to respond with "Kosher."

"Okay, Awesome! We will be sending your flight confirmation and the itinerary in the coming weeks before the trip!" she delivered in her cheerful tone.

I hadn't anticipated that it would be so easy to get a free ten-day trip to Israel. I was curious, but also excited about the potential to explore something that was increasingly becoming part of my identity.

After I was accepted, I inquired among my Jewish friends, both those who had gone and those who had not, about their opinions of the trip. My closest friend said he would never go. Another friend had been a tour guide for them. And all the others who had gone only had one thing to say: "It was great!"

I had visited with my mother's side of the family a few weeks before I applied for the trip. It was during this visit in which it became apparent to me that my mother was raised practicing the Jewish faith, more so than she had let on. My aunt and I had dug through pictures of my mother and father at bar and bat mitzvahs. I found an old picture of my grandfather in a kippah with my grandmother smiling at his side. I was growing more and more attached to the idea that we were Jewish. That I was Jewish.

After I was accepted into the Birthright trip, I decided that perhaps I should do some more self-educating on Jewish culture and Israeli history.

Being Hawaiian, and generally opposed to colonialism of any sort, I had always sympathized with the struggle of Palestinians against the Israeli occupation, but I also felt as though I did not really have a strong grasp of the history of the region. I read a detailed history of Mandate Palestine between the 1920s and 1948, the year Israel was founded as a state. I read about the kibbutzim and their socialist utopian ideology and their struggle to build a new society. I read Theodore Herzl's The Jewish Question and read about the history of the Zionist movement. I uncovered some unsavory accounts of Ben Gurion's colonialism and that of other leaders in the Zionist movement. I asked my close friend from Israel to tell me about her family's history in the country. Her mother was American and her father from a kibbutz in Israel. She chose the United States as her home of the two choices, saying it was a nicer place to be.

I dug through the website of the Anti-Defamation League or ADL, a well-known organization that works to eradicate anti-Semitism. While their mission on paper seems promising, they frequently come under scrutiny for what exactly they consider "anti-Semitism," including in their definition any political statement against the nation-state of Israel. In 2014, the ADL released results from a survey that measured worldwide anti-Semitism. One question from the eleven question survey asked:

"Jews are more loyal to Israel than to this country/country they live in. Is this probably true or probably false?"

New York Magazine slammed the results saying the survey was, "odd and potentially misleading."

One night, I watched *Defamation*, a film about anti-Semitism in the 21st Century from the perspective of an Israeli citizen. The next night I watched *The Ultra Zionists*, a short television documentary by Louis Theroux about Jewish extremist settlements in the West Bank. Despite my efforts to understand the issues surrounding Israel, I was finding that the more I learned, the less I knew for certain.

I was feeling as though my preparations were a good start, but my mother's lingering question was burning in my mind: "What's the catch?"

This question was the seed out of which so many more questions began to grow: What is this trip really about? Did I really have a "birthright?" If so, why? I wanted to understand how the concept of birthright fits into the broader context of the Israeli occupation.

I rummaged through the websites of the Birthright organization and Israel Outdoors, the branch I had chosen to travel through. I still had no clear idea of what the trip was really about or where the funding came from, in spite of my best efforts and questions to veterans of the trip. Most friends who recalled the trip were very ambiguous about its contents. "You have to try this particular ice cream when you're there," one friend unhelpfully advised.

The website for Israel Outdoors had pages of information about what type of shoes to bring, but little about where we would go or what to expect. The organization used the word "gift" profusely in its literature but never clearly unveiled who was giving this gift, only that it was entitled to Jewish people between the ages of 18 and 26.

When the day arrived, I packed my bags for my free trip to the "homeland," but I felt no closer to answers than before.

I had with me the knowledge that there was a strong movement in support of the Palestinians, and at opposition, there was an institution in place to send young American Jews to Israel for free. Whether or not I was really prepared, I remained dedicated to learning more.

Chapter 2: Newark International Airport

I arrived at Newark International airport in New Jersey four hours before our scheduled departure. It was 10 a.m. and the brisk spring morning was filled with sunshine.

Sara had called me a few days before the trip.

"Hey! This is Sara from Birthright! I'll be traveling with you and your group to Israel. Are you excited?!" she asked.

It appeared that her enthusiasm had only inflated.

"I just wanted to let you know that we will be meeting at Newark airport no less than four hours before the flight for check-in and security."

She offered the news in her usual carefree voice.

"Sounds good," I replied, struggling to inject at least half of her excitement into my answer.

Honestly, it didn't sound very good. I considered myself a veteran at flying. Between the year of my long-distance relationship and the year that I played in a cross-country rock band, I had been through dozens of security checkpoints. Four hours seemed like a big time window—until I found out first-hand that security for this trip was a few steps beyond what I was accustomed to.

I had one bag to check in and one carry-on. My usual travel arrangement.

I sauntered through the sliding glass doors of Newark International airport, pausing once I was inside to slip my sunglasses from my nose. I stood facing the El Al desk, Israel's national airline with the tagline, "It's not just an airline. It's Israel." Asserting that I was definitely in the right place, I began walking on, my worn suitcase rolling behind me. I slid my sunglasses onto the neck of my lightweight sweater, perfect for long flights, and meandered at full ease toward the counter where a group of people was cluttered. I walked up behind two girls struggling to keep their oversized suitcases upright while they filled out the check-in sheets. I propped my suitcase against the counter and shifted my eyes to a young woman holding a clipboard and wearing a name tag. She rushed toward me eagerly before I could make out her name.

"Hey! I'm Sara!!" she exclaimed loudly, rippling the waters of my internal calmness.

Her smile was as big as her enthusiasm. She stood gleaning a mouthful of teeth at me, waiting for me to introduce myself.

"I'm Nani," I responded and extended my hand.

We greeted each other kindly and headed over to the counter together. She instructed me to read and sign two papers. One sheet was about having purchased travel insurance and the other was about the rules for alcohol on the trip. No alcohol on the flight. No alcohol before Yad Vashem (the Holocaust museum) and a few more limitations and instructions on alcohol consumption. Nothing that seemed unreasonable.

I put my name on a name tag and hung the big plastic holder around my neck. All the confidence I had as a veteran traveler was waning as I tried to assimilate into the group. I went petering slowly up to two eager faces with name tags for necks. I was about to start a conversation when Sara came up and ushered us all into the line for security, but not airport security. We were all standing in line to go through security for El Al.

Behind a half dozen podiums, El Al airline employees stood with scrutinizing looks and raised eyebrows. Cowering young men and women waiting to be processed stood in front of the podiums. I looked on, feeling my confidence sink even lower. I wondered if this was another test of my Jewish identity.

"Next," grumbled a bearded man in a thick Israeli accent.

I approached, conjuring what was left of my nonchalance for the walk up to my interviewer.

"Passport," he said with his hand out and his face down toward a sheet on the podium.

I handed it to him and waited while he flipped through its pages.

He stopped thumbing when he came to my picture. He glanced up at me, down, up again, then down again.

A moment passed.

Another moment passed.

"What's your name?" he asked, staring at my name.

I smirked, shaking my head slightly.

"Nani Kamalii Kapu Ferreira-Mathews. I know, it's long," I responded.

It wasn't the first time my name had caused some bewilderment. My parents had been creative.

"It's not a Hebrew name," he replied, glancing up condescendingly.

"No. It's Hawaiian," I responded hoping he, like many others before, would find this intriguing.

My attempt to amuse him failed miserably. He moved his eyes from my passport to my face for what felt like a breathless eternity. Finally, moving his head up to look past me, he caught eyes with another employee moving around the floor with an air of importance. Without dismissing or explaining himself, he walked from behind the podium toward the other employee with my passport clenched in his unforgiving fist.

I stood looking forward into the empty space that he had just vacated. I could vaguely see the two men huddle together in my peripheral vision. I tried not to seem suspicious and made a casual peek toward them. It appeared as if they were now both stuck in a perpetual passport to face glance-dance. I stood frozen. My heart was racing. Others who had come to check-in had signed sheets, draped name tags around their necks, answered a few questions at the podium, and were checking in their luggage already. I continued to stand, slouching uncomfortably in front of the empty podium.

My stocky bearded interrogator shuffled slowly back to his place and looked up at me again.

"Do you speak Hebrew?" he asked.

"No, I hope to learn though," I responded hoping to break the question/answer routine with a dialogue.

"Why do you need to learn Hebrew?" he shot back at me without any emotional display.

"Well, I don't need to. I want to. I think it would be helpful," my nervousness was beginning to slip out between my teeth.

"Helpful," he said blankly, staring at me.

I nodded uncomfortably.

"What are you going to Israel for?" he asked.

I was stunned at the question. It was obvious that I was a part of the group of young people traveling for Birthright. I had the name tag to prove it, even if I didn't have a Hebrew name to put on it.

"Birthright." I replied matching his blankness.

If I was hoping to evoke some amusement during this uncomfortable situation, that hope had slipped away by now.

"Are you Jewish?" he threw at me.

"Yes." I replied.

"What holiday did you last celebrate?"

"Passover," I answered.

"With whom did you celebrate?"

"Friends in Brooklyn."

He didn't seem to care about my pleasant meal or my eagerness to commiserate on the huge quantities of matzos consumed.

"Have you been to Israel before?" he asked, breezing on to new topics.

"No."

"Do you know anyone in Israel?"

"Yes," I answered with relief.

I thought that maybe knowing someone there would make this process easier. I have Israeli friends. I can be trusted, right? I had emailed my Israeli friend's sister and I was going to stay with her in Haifa once the Birthright trip was over. Recalling this connection made me smile, but my momentary happiness was quickly sucked dry.

"What's their name?" he asked watching my smile dissipate.

Shit! I thought. I couldn't pronounce her name and I wasn't even sure how it might sound from the signature in the emails. I stood with a nonplus look spread thoroughly across my face.

"I don't remember," I finally admitted.

He looked at me as if he were waiting for a continuation of my answer.

"It's my friend's sister. We never met before," I quickly explained, "I could pull up the email with her name. I'm not really sure how you say it."

I pulled out my phone but it had no signal. I looked up at him in fright. I was beginning to look and feel as if I was seriously suspicious.

I stared at him, my mouth slightly agape in disbelief, as he rushed behind the podium, past me, and toward the same man as before. They stood in consultation for some minutes, staring in my direction and speaking only from behind my open passport.

My mind was racing with all the things I was saying that seemed to be so wrong. I looked around the terminal toward where I met Sara and originally checked-in. I didn't spot her or any familiar faces. I still had over three hours before my flight departed, but I was growing concerned that I would never make it past this podium. Maybe I wasn't Jewish enough for this guy and his slimy-haired boss who stood staring at me. Maybe I wasn't going to Israel. While I was lost among my many concerns, my bearded interrogator returned. He stood silently, flipping through my passport again.

"Why did you visit Ecuador so many times?" he inquired.

I let out a little laugh as I recalled the reason there were five entry and exit stamps when I had only made re-entry once.

"I crossed at a border with no computer and they had a stamp problem," I replied shortly.

It was really a good story, but he didn't give me the impression that he was an appreciator of human haphazardness. He looked up at me briefly after I gave up on the long response, and quickly returned to flipping back and forth, again, through my passport pages.

"You went to Japan," he remarked.

I only nodded.

"Have you ever been to the Middle East?"

"No."

"Do you have any other passports?"

"No. I only have that one."

"It says that you lost your passport and this is a reissue," he said showing me the page where the passport office had printed those exact words.

That was another story, one that wasn't so funny, but still a good one to tell.

"I didn't lose it. The passport office lost it," I replied.

I noticed my frustration was beginning to show in my responses.

He raised his eyebrows as his thumb stopped on yet another page.

"You went to Russia?"

"No. I got the visa, but I never went."

That's another good story about government bureaucracy and incompetence, but I was certain he would not find it amusing.

He looked at me with a deep suspicion and walked off again toward his sidebar consultant.

I was struggling to keep my suitcase from falling over and my sunglasses kept getting tied up with my name tag. My frustration was beginning to show. I was shifting my weight from one leg to the other, remembering how little I had managed to sleep the night before. I was suddenly tired and restless. I felt my face tighten in annoyance. I didn't bother looking at my two judges who were surely standing furtively off in the distance. There was no one else being asked questions behind the podiums beside me. In fact, the other employees had vacated their stations behind the podiums and they were unoccupied on both sides. I stood alone, waiting. I sighed, or huffed in irritation, and shifted my weight again.

Finally, my personal interrogator arrived back in front of my heavy eyes. He continued the never ending flipping through my passport. I was half inclined to tell him to keep it so I could leave the airport and go home and get back in bed.

"Is this the only suitcase you have?" he asked looking at my measly carry-on bag.

"Yes." I responded.

I was hoping this shift was an indicator that I was going to get past this point before infinity had run out.

"Who packed your bag?"

"I did."

"Did anyone help you pack?"

Just a few hours earlier, I had a friend sit on it to help me zip it up. It was very funny then, but not at all funny in this moment.

"No," I answered stoically.

"Are you bringing anything into Israel for anyone?"

"No."

"Did you pack anything that could be used to make a bomb?" he inquired in complete seriousness.

"No."

Actually, I probably did. You can make a bomb out of all kinds of things, but I let my inner jester sit this round out.

After I answered his last question, he came over and began tagging my suitcase, my carry-on, and my handbag with big bright yellow tags. It seemed as if I was going to be allowed to check-in, but with restrictions.

He moved back behind the podium, and placed a yellow sticker with a barcode on the back of my passport.

"How long are you planning to stay in Israel?"

"Three to five months," I replied.

"And this is all you packed?" he said, looking down at my small suitcase.

"Yes. I travel light, and there are clothes in Israel I hope," I answered condescendingly.

There was a pause. I saw him contemplate opening up another round of questions, but he refrained.

"Take your bag over there," he said pointing toward the check-in counter.

I began to wheel it over and quickly noticed that he was right behind me. He watched me put the bag on the conveyor and watched it go down and out of my reach before he handed me a boarding pass and my passport.

"When you go through airport security, we will check your carry-on bags," he said and turned away.

I retreated, as if wounded, out into the vast empty terminal. I still had over two hours before boarding. I sought out a place to sit with a cup of coffee before I proceeded to go through the next two rounds of security.

I dropped myself down into an uncomfortable plastic chair with my bad cup of airport coffee and stared straight ahead. The El Al interrogation did not seem like a random encounter. I was singled out for reasons that were unclear to me. My thoughts fired rapidly at the indications of such an intense screening process before I was handed my boarding pass. It was becoming clear that if I didn't fit into El Al's standards of Jewish identity, then I was seen as a matter of concern for Israel's national security. I raised red flags in what, for many, was a simple process. Was it my name? Was it the uncertainty of whether I was tied to the Middle East or if I was lying? And what authority does an airline have on restricting my movements about the world if I have no legal limitation?

El Al is Israel's national airline and until 2005 was entirely owned by the government. Now privatized, the state of Israel only owns thirteen percent of the airline, but despite its smallholdings, it has the biggest interest in its operation. El Al is world-renowned for being the airline with the highest level of security. It is also renowned for its racial profiling of Arabs and has been in court many times facing these allegations. In 2010, El Al faced a court order for eight thousand dollars in damages after it found the treatment of two Palestinian citizens leaving from New York was "abusive and unnecessary."[1]

El Al employees check passports against databases such as those of the FBI and other international security organizations and will not allow passengers to board flights who do not go through the preliminary interview procedures. It was the most intense security process I had been through, and it was only round one. I got up to make my way toward the airport security checkpoint. That's when I remembered the books I had in my carry-on.

When I had been researching Israeli history, I had become fascinated by the Kibbutzim. I was particularly interested in studying the utopian socialist/anarchist ideology that the original kibbutzim demonstrated. I was extending my trip by three to five months so that I could continue to study kibbutzim models and self-governing social structures in Israel/Palestine. For this research, I had two very helpful resource books: *Fragments of an Anarchist Anthropology* by David Graeber and *A Living Revolution: Anarchism is the Kibbutz Movement* by James Horrox. Unfortunately, they both boldly feature the word anarchy in the titles. It would have been a shame to lose the books, but, hoping to avoid any more unnecessary encounters with El Al security, I decided to dump them in the trash.

I've since discussed this dilemma with many people. Some say, "You should have kept the books. I don't think it would have mattered." Some agree that what I did next was the correct move. I knew that if I threw the books out, I wouldn't have to deal with questions regarding them. However, if I kept them, and if El Al found them in my bag once I got to the other side of airport security, what were the possible courses of action?

It could be that the employees of El Al who looked through my bags wouldn't care. They could be looking for containers of liquid over three ounces. They could be tired and have no concern for anything in my bag at all. However, an El Al employee charged with protecting the Israeli nation-

1 "Israeli Arab brothers win payout for El Al 'abuse' in New York." *The National.* 20 April 2010. http://www.thenational.ae/news/world/middle-east/israeli-arab-brothers-win-payout-for-el-al-abuse-in-new-york

state would almost certainly be suspicious of these titles, or anything that said "anarchy." This is my experience with how most people interpret the word anarchy, an overwhelmingly misunderstood idea that is often received as a threat to security and order. Anarchy, as described by radical feminist Emma Goldman, is no threat to security and order but is rather a "social order based on the free grouping of individuals."[2] For me, that means collective, self-governing, autonomous decision making that is free from the oversight of a large government and militarized nation that has no ears to hear individuals. Most do not see the term in this light.

Throwing two books away seems easy, but after the first round of questions, I still felt as though everyone was watching me, so I kept them in my bag and got up to make a move through airport security. This was the checkpoint I was familiar with. Laptop in the bin, shoes off, walk through the metal detector, hand the boarding pass to the TSA screener, and then reassemble your belongings and outfit. Done.

I threw my backpack over my shoulders and walked toward my gate. I was still on the fence about what to do with the books. I thought that perhaps I misunderstood my interrogator. Maybe they were only going to rummage through my checked bag. I pictured all its contents pouring out when they unzipped it and the carnival that would ensue when two or three uniformed El Al employees shoved my clothes back in, pushed, jumped and sat on the suitcase just to zip it up. That thought was justice enough.

I walked down the long corridor, toward my departure gate. I didn't really know anyone that was in my Birthright group, and I still didn't spot any familiar faces. There were four or five bundles of groups gathered throughout the waiting areas. I walked around looking for someone with my group number on their name tag.

I walked past a rabbi consulting with two young girls about their journey and groups sitting in circles listening attentively to their organizers. Finally, I happened upon my group. It looked like nearly forty young adults sitting on the ground in a circle. I approached slowly and sat down with them. Just as I settled in and began to listen, Sara approached me and whispered,

"El Al needs to see you over there."

She pointed toward an unmarked door with a few seats outside of it.

---

2 Emma Goldman, *Anarchism and Other Essays.* (New York: Dover, 1969), 50.

Rushing with anxiety I quickly asked, "I really need to use the bathroom. Can I do that first?"

"Um," she hesitated, "Sure, just hurry. They've been waiting for you."

They have been waiting for me? I wondered as I hurried toward the bathroom. I pushed my way into a stall and grabbed the books out of my bag, my two most valuable resources on this trip. I had marked notes and written other resources I needed to supplement them with. I shook my head as I pushed them deep into the trash can.

They are just things, I thought, reassuring myself over the loss.

I came out of the stall, flushing the toilet for effect before I opened the door. An El Al employee stood adjusting her hair in the mirror and caught eyes with me. I broke our gaze and washed my hands quickly before rushing over to the unmarked door for my bag search.

I sat down in an empty chair and waited. The morning was much more intense than I had anticipated. I was already mentally exhausted from the interrogation and now I was waiting to be probed even further. I was looking forward to getting through this part and sleeping on the ten-hour flight. That was the light at the end of this bureaucratic tunnel.

I heard my name over the intercom.

"Please report to gate thirty-seven or see an El Al employee," the voice ordered.

I went to stand up when the door behind me opened.

"Are you Nani Ferreira?" a uniformed man asked, butchering the pronunciation from the crack in the door.

"Yes," I said, standing.

"Sit down," he quickly ordered, "We will be with you in a minute."

The door slammed shut as he disappeared behind it.

I sat, holding my mouth tight in aggravation.

I was looking over toward my group. They were playing some sort of icebreaker game. I was suddenly unsure that being in that circle was any better than being interrogated and bossed around by grumpy airline employees.

The door opened again breaking my internal dialogue and scattering my thoughts.

"Come in, please," the young man said.

On the other side of the door were more chairs.

"Sit down. If you have any money in your bags, take it out now," he ordered.

He stood watching me closely as I removed my passport holder and my wallet. I handed him my two bags and he disappeared behind a curtain.

Two other people were already sitting in the room when I arrived. They remained quiet, but looked like they too had a rough time already.

There was an old tube television playing reruns of *Friends* with no sound and closed captions. On the table in front of me, there were out of date *Elle* and *In Style* magazines. I chuckled to myself. Perhaps this is some form of Israeli torture, I thought. I felt pretty tortured watching Courtney Cox bounce around the television screen in a now-vintage 90s jumper.

There was lots of shuffling behind the screen as they dug through my belongings. After some minutes, the same young man reemerged with a blue plastic brush in his hand. I raised my eyebrows at him in silent question.

He kneeled in front of me, without explanation, and began to swab my shoes. I sat still, looking on at him in disbelief. The security measures I was going through seemed excessive, and they put on *Friends* as a means to still my worried soul. Disbelief may be too light of a word for what I was feeling.

He rose quietly and disappeared behind the curtain again.

A moment passed.

Another moment passed.

Finally, he came out holding my bags at arms length in latex gloves and handed them back to me.

Removing the gloves and throwing them in the trash he said, "Come with me," to me and the two who were there before me.

We walked out of the room and directly up to the gate. The flight was not scheduled to board for another twenty minutes.

"Boarding pass," said the gate employee.

I had no idea what was going on or why we were the only ones being ushered toward the gate. I handed her my boarding pass and passport. Without looking up, she scanned my boarding pass and asked me to board.

I moved slowly down the extendable corridor. I wasn't sure if I was relieved that I was on the flight or not. Once I got to the aircraft, a flight stewardess directed me to my seat. I slid into my place by the window and buckled up. There was movement on the aircraft, but from what I could tell, it wasn't being boarded yet.

I took out my phone, attended to a text message and turned it off, then leaned my head back against my seat. I wanted to text my friends about the trip so far, but I was afraid I was under some surveillance. I had no books to read and was feeling very tired. I attempted to nod off but was stirred awake when the other passengers began boarding.

As we made our way into the air, I found peace in knowing I could rest my mind before we arrived in Israel. Unfortunately, I soon realized that everyone else on the flight was planning to spend the next ten hours performing an impromptu J-Date mixer.[3]

As soon as the "Fasten Seatbelt" sign went off, boys got up and headed toward girls, girls got up and headed toward boys, rounds of young people gathered in the aisles and huddled around rows having a hundred conversations. It seemed that the air of discomfort that had started this trip was to remain a running theme through the entire thing.

I sat with my head back in exhaustion hoping I wouldn't get sucked into any of the conversations around me.

Ten hours until Tel Aviv.

---

3 J-Date is the "World's premiere Jewish dating site," according to their website. The organization and its members also host a number of events worldwide that encourage interfaith dating. These events are sometimes referred to as "J-Date mixers."

Chapter 3: Haifa and Speed Dating

"Thirty-seven! Thirty-eight! Thirty-nine!"

We finished our first count off and stood crowded around the baggage carousel. We were not quite forty.

I swayed with exhaustion and squinted as the early morning light poured through the glass windows of Ben Gurion International Airport in Tel Aviv. We had each been assigned a number to count off with so our two staff members could keep track of us.

"How many girls and how many boys?" I heard Sara whisper over the shoulder of our other staff member who was holding the clipboard.

"It's almost split down the middle," she replied.

The two girls exchanged a look of mischief and smiled.

These were our two facilitators for the trip, Sara and Amy.

They were responsible for keeping us out of trouble and helping us get to know each other. I found out later that they were not being paid to facilitate the ten-day trip, but were volunteering their time in return for a free trip to Israel.

Sara stood an inch or two over five feet tall and had a constant look of cheer in her big brown eyes. Her mouth, always slightly open, was a resting hand on a smile holster.

Amy had a familiar face, inviting, bright, and polished. She had a full head of curly, bouncy brown hair. Her eyes were the type of blue that were so blue they stunned you at how blue they were. She had high cheekbones and pursed lips. Despite being clad in a Birthright t-shirt, gym shorts, and tennis shoes, she carried herself with a sense of privileged elegance.

We were quickly corralled and told we had ten minutes to change into clothes appropriate for hiking. I looked around at everyone digging through their suitcases next to the baggage claim. I was too exhausted and heavy lidded to bother opening my suitcase. I took the ten minutes to buy a cup of coffee and gather myself. I thought that the day would start slowly. We lost nearly twenty four hours between the travel time and the time difference, and we were standing on the other side of the world in the next day. We were a little disoriented, to say the least.

The ten minutes we were given to change clothes and money flew by like ten seconds and we were being pushed out into the humid Israeli air and onto our coach bus.

It was just past 8:00 a.m. and we were promised a full day ahead as we threw our luggage under the coach and boarded. I took a seat in the front, out of pure fatigue, and stared out the window longing for sleep.

Before I knew it, we were pulling out of the airport and driving toward a full list of activities on our soon-to-be-announced agenda.

Coincidentally, I sat next to our two staff members, Sara and Amy, who were shuffling through papers and consulting with our tour guide and guard in the seat ahead of me about the day's events.

"How many boys and how many girls?" asked our tour guide.

"Almost half and half," answered Sara, smiling with excitement.

I wondered why this question kept coming up.

Our tour guide stood in the aisle and fumbled with the bus microphone. He was a slim and dark middle-aged Israeli man, adorned with a kippah and a look of modesty in his eyes. He resembled a turtle with its neck extended when he wasn't keeping his posture in mind.

"Shalom, and welcome to Israel," he started once he got the mic working.

There were some shouts of sleepy excitement from the back of the bus. I sat staring out the window wide-eyed and slipping into deliriousness.

"We have a busy day ahead of us," he began. "First, we'll stop and have breakfast on a kibbutz, then we will visit the Bahá'í Gardens in Haifa. After that, we will take a nature walk to a beautiful lookout point over the Sea of Galilee, take a lunch break in Tiberius, and finally we will bus to a kibbutz in the Galilee and settle in for the night."

I snapped my stare from the Israeli landscape and at our tour guide. Nowhere in that day was there a moment to breathe or brush our teeth. It didn't sound like we would have a break until it was over. I suddenly wasn't sure what I had got myself into, but before I had time to contemplate it at all, our tour guide was back in the microphone.

"There are packets being passed around for you all," he announced, "and in them there is a map of Israel so you can see where we've been and where we are going."

He said this as he struggled to hang the map from a line in the middle of the aisle and began dropping the microphone to the bus floor. Our armed guard rushed up to help him juggle the two items. It was the first time I noticed the gun on our guard's hip.

Every Birthright tour provides an armed guard. We had only been in the country a few hours, but it didn't feel as though we needed armed protection.

Unfolding the map so it was hanging in the aisle for everyone to see, Shai began to show us where we would be going for the day.

"Israel is very small, as you can see from this map. We will cover a lot of the country in just a few hours. It's the same size as New Jersey," he said.

There is always mention of how small Israel is in comparison to its neighbors. I've been to small countries before and have never heard them try to relate themselves to small states in the U.S.

"First, we will be going to Haifa to visit the Bahá'í Gardens. The Bahá'í are a small religious group and make up a minimal amount of the population of Israel."

"Haifa, the city we will visit with the Bahá'í gardens has a very mixed population. Arabs, Christians, and Jews populate this metropolis," Shai informed us.

Haifa, I thought. I knew that's where my friend's sister lived. The one whose name I didn't know during my interrogation. There was something else, though. Why did that city sound so familiar?

As I looked at the map they had handed out I noticed that there was no border drawn around the West Bank. There was a small gray block where the Gaza Strip is located. No cities or sites were mentioned. It simply read, "Gaza Area." However, there was no mention, of any kind, of the West Bank. No partition lines around Jerusalem. The map suggested that all of the West Bank was in fact Israel. I looked for a map legend or any explanation without any luck.

Again, my thoughts were interrupted. We pulled into the kibbutz where we would have breakfast and begun unloading and filing into the dining room.

I sat off to myself, mostly to produce unhindered thoughts, but I was quickly joined by a few others in my group. It was apparent since the flight that the people on this trip were in the mood to socialize. It was futile to resist the conversation, but I remained a bystander as long as I could while it closed in around me.

We ate quickly and were all back on the bus within an hour.

As we drove toward Haifa I began to doze. There was an empty seat beside me and the low mumbles of the staff on the other side of the aisle. The inaudible conversations throughout the bus were my lullaby. I awoke in Haifa.

Our bus driver maneuvered through the slim city streets with confidence and ease. He demonstrated his skills fearlessly and appeared to know every street before we ever got to it. I wondered how many times he had driven a bus through this city. How many groups of kids had he chauffeured through Israel? I wondered what he thought about the thirty-nine of us on his bus, muttering ungratefully in English about the bad food on the kibbutz.

He pulled around without effort to the top of the gardens and let us out. As I stepped outside the bus, I realized how much hotter it was here than it was in New York, and it was not even noon yet. My sleepiness was not fading, despite a quick nap. My head and body were heavy under the burning sun. I slipped my sunglasses on and shuffled along slowly with our large group.

We all followed Shai, our tour guide, as he crossed the road toward the narrow sidewalk overlooking the gardens. I stood looking down the finely manicured gardens while the rest of our group crowded in. The view was magnificent, but I only enjoyed it for a brief moment. Before I knew it, I was pressed firmly against a railing and a dozen bodies with arms extending cameras.

I slipped to the back of the pack, still struggling to find my own thoughts.

Shai encouraged us to take pictures as he started talking about the Bahá'í religion. He mentioned the importance of religious tolerance and the diversity of religion within the city of Haifa. The Bahá'í, he explained, was a religious group that was a part of Israel before the Jewish people declared independence and founded a state for their people to return to.

There were a few things plaguing me about this place. Haifa had a spot in my memory, but between exhaustion and delirium, I was having trouble accessing it.

Shai did not elaborate on the Bahá'í religion or any of their customs. He did not speak much of their history, and only shared a sentence or two about the religion before the time that Israel became a nation. He spoke mostly of the garden and how it was a great attraction for the tourism industry of Haifa.

We stood, nearly forty young adults, crowded onto a thin sidewalk in the blazing sun, overlooking a magnificent garden kept by a religious group I know nothing more about now than before I had ever heard of it. Remembering back on it, I could only tell you that their presence supposedly demonstrated how religiously tolerant people are in Israel. At least, that was the message that our guide was giving us.

Shai continued to talk about Haifa and how many different religions coexisted in the city harmoniously. He stood in front of us, moving his arms around like a magician and letting his posture slip and transform him into a hungry turtle.

I began to zone out and leaned over the railing I was once pressed against. Looking out past the gardens I could see the ocean. The shoreline. That's when it hit me like a crashing wave.

Haifa.

I remembered why it stuck out to me.

We were standing on Mt. Carmel overlooking the ocean. This was the place where during the Israeli War of Independence in 1948, nearly sixty thousand Palestinians were forcefully pushed out of the city and toward ships waiting in the harbor to export them.

I remembered reading about this slope we were perched upon. The Jewish army utilized this geographic vantage point to push Palestinian civilians out of Haifa and into the port. Thousands of Palestinians who were working and living in Haifa before Jewish settlers arrived were violently forced out of their homes. The Carmeli Brigade stationed mortars on the slope to shower the fleeing population from the hillside. Throughout an entire day, the Brigade used mortars to shell the crowds in the market square and force Arabs to evacuate. Boats at the port became so overcrowded with refugees that many sank.

"Haifa is still a mixed population where Arabs, Jews, and Christians all live and work together, and is Israel's third largest city."

Shai was wrapping up his hilltop speech. There was a gentle applause from those paying attention, but most of us were not. I was beginning to think that maybe it wasn't such a bad thing to zone out of these speeches.

We were suddenly back on the bus. I still had an empty seat beside me and stretched my legs out. I was preparing to nod off before our next adventure when I heard a nasally female voice cut through the speakers.

"Hey guys!" Sara hissed into the microphone that she was holding far too close to her mouth.

I shook the sleep from my ears and sat up to hear the announcement.

"It's time for another icebreaker, and this one's a good one!" she exclaimed.

There was some excitement, but the general response was grogginess.

I looked over at Sara and Amy just in time to witness the two girls exchange the most scheming glance.

"Can someone give me a drum roll please?" Sara shouted.

People began drumming on the backs of the padded bus seats and producing a thunderous and muffled drum roll.

Intoxicated by the sound, Sara smiled wide before shouting, "It's time for bus speed dating!"

I felt my face make the most judgmental arrangement possible. My lips pressed tightly together. My right eyebrow raised in disbelief and annoyance.

"Here's how it works," she continued, not phased in the least by my clear disdain.

"Boys, you're going to move after each round. We'll go clockwise. Are you ready, guys!?" she cheered.

I sat, thoroughly uncomfortable with anyone assuming that I was in the mood for speed dating, or that I was single in the first place, or that I was interested in dating anyone on this trip.

Hill overlooking the Ba'Hai gardens to the coastline. Haifa.

It dawned on me in this moment why there was such a curiosity in the boy to girl ratio. I hadn't thought about it before. The mingling on the plane and the eagerness of everyone to get to know each other suddenly made sense. How had I not noticed this before?

I had been on trips, backpacked, and hostel-jumped before. I had experienced the culture of the casual traveler hook-up, but the indications here ran much deeper. We weren't casual travelers making consensual adult decisions. It seemed more like we were being coerced. I suddenly felt sick.

Mathematically, it looks like this: Israel has roughly a seventy-five percent Jewish, twenty percent Arab, and four to five percent other population breakdown, with approximately eighty million in its entire population.

In 1948, when Jews officially settled in what is now Israel and pushed out the Palestinian population, between 700,000 and 900,000 Arabs became refugees. In the sixty-five years since this, those forced to leave have made families in occupied Palestine and neighboring countries and roughly total five million registered refugees, according to the United Nations Relief and

Works Agency for Palestine Refugees. If five million Palestinians were able to return home, the population in Israel would about fifty percent Jewish and fifty percent Arab. This number would make it hard to enforce the laws of a Jewish state when half the population does not follow Judaism. Therefore, it's in Israel's best interest to encourage young Jews like us to shack up, move to Israel, and make a ton of Jewish babies. Just in case the day ever comes when those nearly five million refugees get to come home.

The game proceeded.

"Alright, first question," Sara said grinning from ear to ear. "If you had to live off of one type of canned food for the rest of your life, what would it be?"

I heard pairs of voices discuss the hypothetical apocalypse question with true sincerity. I still had an empty seat beside me for the first round. Anxiety began to creep up on me. Why did the first icebreaker have to be a sexual insinuation? I felt ostracized and downcast by the heteronormative implications of this speed dating game.

Sara and Amy were both propped up on their knees and turned around in their seats, eyes on the group. The two girls giggled to themselves as they looked out toward the back of the bus. I sat cowering beside them. I hoped that perhaps no one would make their way into the empty seat beside me. I didn't have a huge problem being coerced into getting to know someone with icebreaker games. However, I did have a serious qualm with being asked to take part in a game with this kind of insinuated intimacy without my consent.

My heart was not on the market, and the assumption that it was up for grabs by some nice young Jewish boy was frustrating. Was it understood that everyone on this trip was single, or even heterosexual for that matter? There were surely others on the bus who felt the stinging of exclusion from this innocuous game.

"Okay, boys, move seats," Sara ordered. "Next questionnnn," she said moaning the last syllable and letting it ring out for a few seconds too long. "If you had a superpower, what would it be?"

I turned to the boy who had just settled down in the seat beside me. I could tell he was shorter than I was even though we were sitting. He had a slight hint of enthusiasm in his eyes, although it was nearly hidden behind his dirty glasses.

"I think I'd be a mind reader," he said smiling. "What about you?"

I was struggling to find conversational words through the strong feelings of opposition I was having toward this game. Somehow, I managed to spit out some nonsense.

"Uh, I guess I'd fly. I'm not really sure," I mumbled.

"I'm Ben. What's your name?" he asked gently.

"Nani."

"Whoa, that's an interesting name," he responded.

"It's not Hebrew," I offered sarcastically.

"I think you say mint in Hebrew, 'nana,'" he replied smiling.

"That's good to know," I said quickly.

There was a quiet that fell between us. His eyes shifted back and forth as he scoured his brain for another line of dialogue, but it was too late.

"Boys, move!" screamed Sara.

As Ben went to leave I said, "Hey, I think a better superpower is to make people shit themselves."

He looked at me perplexed and turned away.

The gravel moaned loudly beneath our feet as we approached the lookout on top of Mount Arbel. The air was dense and moist and the visibility was low as we exited the bus and walked up the path.

The landscape in Israel had been on the verge of impressive, but it wasn't quite there. Rolling hills were colored with greys and browns. The blue sky was dashed with a misty grey fog hanging on the horizon. It seemed to lack color.

We gathered around Shai as the wind nearly blew the kippah off his head and over the side of the mountain. Again, the cameras came out and people started asking other people to take pictures of them standing in Israel.

I took a seat on a flat rock and let the wind take my hair wildly wherever it wished.

Shai began to speak about the lookout and the importance of Mount Arbel to history of the Jewish people. He spoke of the Druze, another religious group that populated this region of Israel.

"Not much is known about the Druze, and their customs are sworn to secrecy," he said. "The Druze were in Israel as far back as the second temple, but still little is known about their culture," he continued. "During the War of Independence many Druze decided to join the Jewish army, and in return were granted citizenship when Israel was formed."

He went on but my mind drifted. It was nearly sunset. We had been moving nonstop since sometime thirty-six hours ago on a different continent. I was fatigued and jet-lagged beyond description. I could have fallen asleep sitting on that rock with the wind in my hair.

I heard Shai clear his throat in a way that grabbed my attention. He had shifted topics and for the first time, he seemed to be speaking to us and not at us. His voice softened to reflect this change.

"Listen," he began earnestly, "I am going to be with you for the next ten days. We are going to see a lot of places, very fast. This country is my home. It's where I was born and where I was raised. I served in the military when I was younger and I've become more religious as I've become older. I love this country," he paused dramatically. "Some of you have a strong Jewish background and some of you don't. Either way, you are all here because this is your home. It's your right to be here in the Jewish homeland. I hope that I can show you the beauty of this country and that you can feel connected to your heritage."

He looked slowly onto all the faces in front of him, making eye contact with us, one at a time. He had a captive audience and was pushing us to connect our Jewish identity to the state of Israel.

Speaking slowly, he continued, "Our people suffered injustice after injustice. This is our home. We've been through many wars to defend it. We will visit the graves of only a few of the many national heroes that were lost so that you could be standing here today."

He smiled intensely and lifted his arms in offering.

"Welcome home!" he shouted, his voice bellowing and landing with triumph on the ears of his audience.

There was a loud burst of applause from our group. Nearly everyone was moved to applaud his second mountaintop speech of the day. I golf clapped for the delivery. It was quite a spectacle. However, I didn't feel like I was home. In fact, I was wondering why I, with so little Jewish background, would be welcomed home here. I identified with my family's heritage. I longed to hear more about my great-great grandparents lives as Jewish immigrants to New York in the early 1900s. I wanted to know more about the traditions of Judaism that my grandmother, whom I loved beyond words, brought into my mother's life.

Still, I felt uneasy. Despite my emotional ties and my curiosity, I was not clear how this was my rightful "home," especially after remembering how so many of the indigenous people living here before 1947 were forced to leave their land and their homes, much like the forced displacement experienced by some of my ancestors.

We walked back to the bus with the weight of a thousand nights' sleep pressing on our backs. No one walked fully erect, or as if they were of sound body. I sauntered along the gravel path and kicked rocks for both amusement and to keep myself from sleepwalking.

I looked up and into the horizon one last time before I boarded the bus. A tree in the foreground caught my eye. It was bursting wildly with lavender flowers. This was the first color I spotted in the landscape and, even so, it appeared with elusiveness.

Chapter 4: The Mikvah

It was the second day of our trip and we were on the bus toward Tzfat, a nearby town in the northern part of Israel. According to Shai, Tzfat was well known for Jewish mysticism and kabbalah. Contemporary kabbalah practices were made popular by celebrities like Madonna and Gwyneth Paltrow and stirred some excitement among our urban dwellers.

We left the bus and started walking down the narrow marble path. The rubber soles of my oxfords slipped on the polished cobblestone streets as we walked through the ancient city. The stout stone buildings seemed to tower above us in the thin alleyways and swallowed us between the tight corridors.

It was a beautiful old place reminiscent of Florentine and Italian Renaissance architecture. The stone brick walls were colored peach and speckled with whites and browns. Old iron-barred windows had been painted a vibrant turquoise blue and stood out sharply in contrast to their neutral background.

We walked, with care, up and down marble stairs in the center of the city. Before we descended down one particular alley, Shai stopped to mention that it was in this alley that the messiah was expected to ascend from. Of course, everyone stopped to take a picture.

Unfortunately, on this tour there was little more to be learned of kabbalah than one might have already known from its pop culture followers. Our tour guide had little interest or knowledge in Jewish mysticism, and the spiritual lecture he planned on giving us was cut short due to the massive influx of other tourist groups pushing us forward.

When we arrived around 9:00 a.m., the city was fairly unpopulated. But within an hour, the alleyways and streets were bustling with busloads of groups like ours. Whoever actually lived in the city did not appear to be moving around in it. There was only group after group of tourists as far as the eye could see.

Our group got funneled out of the streets and into a square with food vendors. Coincidentally, it was just in time for lunch. As I walked freely around the square, I realized that we had started on the other side of it without realizing it. We had barely moved at all. It felt like we had walked through so many of the streets and alleys, but we had really only made a small circle and ended up almost back where we started. I looked around, watching scores of teens and young adults exchange shekels for falafels and hamsa souvenirs. I wondered what this place would look like if busloads of organized groups did not arrive here every morning. It would be a ghost town without us, I presumed.

I wasn't hungry. I took a seat on a bench and watched what appeared to be the only commerce in the small ancient city.

A guy from my group sat on the bench beside me with a hat on his face and his head leaned back. He began to stir not long after I sat down. Straightening himself, he placed his old and worn New York Yankees cap back on his head.

He stared out among the bustling square and we sat quietly for a long time. Eventually, forgetting he was there, I fell deep in my own thoughts.

"You're not hungry either, I guess?" he finally said.

I looked over at him for the first time. He looked as tired as I still felt from the previous day.

"No," I responded, "I think I'm still really jetlagged."

"Yeah, and yesterday was so busy, I feel like a zombie," he said chuckling.

I nodded in agreement.

We both continued to watch the swarms of people doing business in the square.

"You think our tour guide gets free lunch here?" he asked.

"Ha! I think he should," I responded without looking over.

"Yeah, I bet he brings hundreds of people here every year and those hundreds of people buy hundreds of falafels. He should get a free falafel," he said chuckling again.

"Yeah, or a free 'I Love Israel' t-shirt," I said joining his laughter.

"Who lives here?" he asked aloud to no one in particular.

"I don't think anyone actually lives here," I said answering him, "I think all these guys just bring in their hamsa necklaces and falafel carts before we get here and then leave after we leave. They probably all live in Tel Aviv," I said laughing to myself.

"I'm Brian," he said looking over toward me.

"Hey Brian, I'm Nani," I responded and nodded toward him.

I spotted Shai on the other side of the square waving his hands in the air trying to herd his flock away from the others.

Brian and I stood and joined our group as we all left the square.

Shai gave us our next instructions once we were all together.

"Girls, you are going to go with Sara and Amy and boys will come with me," Shai directed us once we were out of the bustling square.

"We'll come back here afterward and head back to the kibbutz to prepare for dinner," he said.

I had no idea what to expect as I fell in line with the rest of my assigned gender group. We began to follow Sara and Amy around a large sand-colored limestone building with no signs to suggest where we were headed.

We entered into a quiet and intimately lit foyer. As I looked around, I noticed shelves and tables of merchandise. Wedding plates and fragile elaborate gifts lined the walls. Where were we? I thought.

A door on the other side of the foyer/gift shop opened and a rosy-cheeked woman emerged smiling.

"Hello," she said gently and with an American accent.

She wore a flowery skirt down to the floor and a loose fitting white button up blouse. Her hair was covered in a beautiful teal scarf with elaborate gold stitching. Her face was bright and welcoming and she exuded confidence.

"Welcome," she said softly. "Please come in."

She opened the doorway she was standing in so that we could pass through. On the other side was an immaculately decorated lounge. Plush chairs and couches were all facing a huge glass coffee table on a polished silver frame. We took our seats with care. There were sitting pillows and throw pillows all along the couches.

"Get comfortable," our gentle hostess whispered as she too moved softly through the space.

She joined our circle and took a seat among us. She smiled warmly and let the air fall to silence for just enough time to offer us relaxation. There was a peace that filled the room. It was clean and comfortable. It smelled like flowers, but was not overwhelming to the senses. The light was soft. The chairs were soft. Our hostess was soft.

"Ladies," she began, "welcome to Israel."

Subtle smiles appeared on relaxed faces. We had all been moving so quickly and had been pushed through crowded streets and alleys all morning. This gentle moment was priceless. I smiled too.

"My name is Avagail," she began, "and today we are going to talk about girl stuff," she said with sass.

Despite her Orthodox clothing and soft voice, she still maintained a hint of an American attitude. She was originally from New York.

"This room is very special. It is a room for women only and it is one of our wedding rooms," she explained.

It was a space that reminded me of American wedding décor. The walls were covered in soft blue wallpaper with silver paisley etchings. Everything in the room was placed cleanly and hinted at purity.

"Many Jewish women come here to have bridal showers and to commune among their sisters before taking the vows of marriage," she said looking at each of us.

"Who here is married?" she asked.

Two girls raised their hands.

Avagail smiled, "Masel Tov, we rarely ever have married women in Birthright groups."

I privately wondered why that is.

"These two ladies may know already know the answer to my next question," she continued. "Have any of you ever heard of a mikvah?" she asked furtively.

A few girls raised their hands, including myself. I read about mikvahs when an old one was unearthed in a New York City construction project on the Lower East Side. I read that it was a ritualistic bath, but I did not know much else.

Avagail looked at us gently smiling.

"Today, we are going to talk about the mikvah and women in Judaism," she continued vaguely. "This building we are in is a mikvah and it's place for women of the Jewish faith to come and really channel their femininity," she said pressing her palms together in a meditative pose.

Our hostess was delivering her sentences at a snail's pace. She spoke in the soft affirming tone of new age guru and nodded her head when she spoke. She put her elbows to her knees and leaned in closer. She remained in this posture, smiling and nodding; she made eye contact with all of us women in the circle.

"Sometimes," she continued, "women just need a break from men. Am I right, ladies?" she said laughing.

The girls in the circle laughed with her and confirmed with hoots. I recall at least one, "Amen," coming from an unknown direction.

"A mikvah is a spiritual escape, where only women are allowed. It's a place where I personally come to relax," she said bobbing her head again.

She unfolded her pose and sat back upright.

"But ladies," she began, "we do love our men too, right?" she asked nodding in sincerity.

Again, at least one "amen" was shouted out.

I wasn't quite sure what Avagail was uncovering, but she was surely popular with all the heterosexual women in the room. I saw our one self-identified bisexual group member looking on with a degree of uncertainty.

"I love my husband," she said holding her heart, "so much that I gave him seven children," she said with a proud smile.

Awe and laughter lifted from the circle.

"But sometimes, I just need to spend some time with myself," she said with a sigh.

Avagail continued to describe her deep love for her husband and children for some minutes. She was the first orthodox Jewish woman I had ever heard speak about her love life. After only five or six dates, she and her husband agreed to be married. According to their strong beliefs, they did not even touch before they took the vows of marriage. They never touched hands or touched lips. They went on five dates and were married within a few months.

She explained that the consequences for failing to adhere to these strict guidelines and beliefs could result in immense shame and that marriage is the only way to remain pure.

Avagail segued from delivering this more conservative viewpoint to touting her religion's support of an empowered female.

"Jewish women," she said, "are strong women. We work hard for our families and our home, in return, our men are supposed to provide us with three things in marriage; clothing, a home to decorate, and sex."

She continued by explaining gender segregation at Jewish temple. She told us that men and women are separated during religious services so that men can concentrate on the word of God without being distracted by women.

"It's hard for men to concentrate on the word of God when women are present, and God is above all," she said. "Men adorn themselves with kippahs and women do not because men are more likely to forget God is above them. Women, in the Orthodox religion, are not allowed to be rabbis so that there is no chance a man will be turned on during services," she explained humorously.

Avagail was attempting to prove her case by discrediting its counterpart and, in doing so she was using the oldest fallacy in the book of logical debate, ad hominem.

Women are better than men because men are stupid or cannot control themselves.

To me, it seemed Avagail was not demonstrating women's power in Judaism by her examples, she was simply attacking men as to distract from our perceptions of gender inequality.

I personally did not feel very empowered by her argument, but looking around the room, I got the feeling that I was the only cynic.

She continued, "I cover my head so that my husband will be the only one to see my hair, so that no other man will be tempted to covet my beauty, which is my husband's alone. I love him and I want to remain pure for him in our marriage."

As Avagail continued to talk about the women's role in Orthodox Judaism, it became clear that she was presenting this particularly for women operating from a liberal American perspective.

Avagail, a native New Yorker, had been living in Israel after making Aliyah less than twenty years ago. There were many things about her lifestyle that were greatly different than most every woman on our trip. Nearly everyone on my Birthright tour lived in New York City and was likely leading a very fast-paced urban liberal lifestyle.

Even though her arguments struck me as illogical, one might feel after hearing them that her strict faith gives her power and freedom. Avagail, originally from America, bridged the gap between liberal American culture and orthodox Israeli women with her ability to connect intimately with us. This unique combination created a sympathetic view toward the gender politics of Orthodox Judaism while cleverly leaving the many similarities between more strict Jewish and Muslim practices unmentioned, probably for nationalistic reasons.

We continued away from this topic and onto a tour of the Mikvah. A mikvah is, essentially, a bath of water that some Jewish women, particularly Orthodox women, visit each month after their menstrual cycle. It is a spiritual and physical cleansing.

Avagail explained that there is a one week a month of the female cycle and one week after it for attending the mikvah and cleansing before husband and wife can return to having sex. It is a ritual followed to maintain family purity.

While it is a practice used mostly by Haredi women, I was very surprised to learn that attending a mikvah is a requirement before any marriage in Israel. It is Jewish law that a woman, in preparation for her wedding, should attend a mikvah and be cleansed before entering into marriage. I wondered what that meant for Arab or Christian Israelis. Why would they want anything to do with a spiritual Jewish bath? Unfortunately, it turned out, that it isn't a problem, because in Israel, you are not getting married unless you are Jewish anyways. Israel will only recognize marriages between its Jewish citizens performed by authorized rabbis. That means your best friend's online ordination is no good in Israel. Even more, if you are a Jew marrying a non-Jew, or protestant marrying protestant, or Arab, Muslim or not, you are out of luck. No marriages are recognized by the state of Israel unless they are between two Jews and performed by authorized rabbis.

Chapter 5: Shabbat on the Kibbutz

It was our third day and we had been properly worn out with activity after activity. Luckily, it was Shabbat. On Birthright, it's customary to remain grounded for Shabbat and not use the bus or go anywhere that requires automobiles. For us, that meant, being on the kibbutz for the day, hearing lecture after lecture.

We took a slow mid-morning stroll along the kibbutz as Shai narrated our walk. He gave us a brief history on the kibbutz movement, stating that it was in the kibbutzim that Israel's first settlers arrived to the homeland.

We walked on through the households as he described the turn of kibbutzim from socialist models to more privatized models. Housing was once very communal, with many members of kibbutzim sharing resources and homes. Since the 1980s the kibbutz model has shifted greatly from socialist communal viewpoints to a more individualistic outlook. Homes, once occupied by many, were now only filled with single families. The communal dining rooms were shut down or, as in our kibbutz, used only to feed tourist groups.

Shai did a decent job of a quick general history, but there was also a lot he did not mention about the kibbutz movement.

Before leaving the U.S. I made plans to stay in Israel after the Birthright trip had ended, to observe and study kibbutzim structures and to uncover any anarchist organizational models they may be using. Reading through some books about the kibbutz movement, I found that many were founded with an anarchistic ideology. That is to say, they worked together to make decisions without voting systems or elections. However, as we strolled through the quiet kibbutz in the Galilee I saw that growth and privatization had undermined any anarchist models once used. Nowadays, a kibbutz is like a homeowners association. Families have their own homes that they have a mortgage on. There may be communal spaces, like a pool or playground, but it is less and less common that kibbutz members are eating any meals together.

Author James Horrox in his book, *A Living Revolution: Anarchy in the Kibbutz Movement*, presumed that some kibbutz members, prior to the formation of Israel, were hopeful for a new type of society, governed directly by the people. A society without the same kinds of hierarchical government that many Jews were fleeing from in the first place.

Unfortunately, we know that Zionism would come to form a government much like those that once ostracized Jews, and instead, it would ostracize a different group of people, indigenous Palestinians, in the interest of creating a Jewish State.

Before the formation of Israel in 1948, some early kibbutzim earned their living off of small businesses and farming and remained self-sufficient. After 1948, the emergence of a new state meant development and the need for perceived progress. New businesses brought in so much competition that many kibbutzim began to lose money. The kibbutzim began to flounder in debt, relying increasingly on loans and eventually government support. This led to many kibbutzim privatizing, selling their plots off like a Florida suburb, and thus becoming little boxes on the hillside.

Those are only some of the parts that Shai left out in his brief history.

Further, while I personally enjoy tales of solidarity that come from early kibbutz accounts, it must be remembered that many of these kibbutz settlers were assuming rights to Palestinian land. They were soldiers of a settler-colonialist project, taking land away from Palestinians by way of transfer. That is, driving the indigenous population out of their homeland, their birthright.

David Ben Gurion, Israel's first prime minister and a lead force in the establishment of the state, candidly remarked, "I am for compulsory transfer; I do not see anything immoral in it."

The Jewish National Fund, established at the 1901 Fifth Zionist Congress, was formed to fund land purchases in Palestine and build Jewish settlements. These settlements, often becoming kibbutzim or moshavs, were an early incarnation of the Zionist plan for Palestinian transfer.

Zionist propaganda posters in the early 20th century used headlines such as the popular "Help him build Palestine" poster, which featured a Jewish settler tilling the land. Eager young Zionists, in a myriad of youth movements, were trained in basic agricultural skills and sent to Palestine to join one of the many settlements. These young bodies would face harsh conditions, including bad sanitation, disease, poor harvests, and an increasingly angry and disenfranchised indigenous population—a population that Zionism and kibbutzim were working toward "transferring" to anywhere else, all in the name of establishing a Jewish State.

I waited for an opportunity to bring this up during our walk with Shai, but he maintained a pace, both walking and talking, that left no room for questions.

* * *

We had just finished lunch and were being ushered into a big room to partake in an "afternoon activity." It was that sleepy time of day, right after a big meal when the sun is shining warmly and encouraging the world to go rest.

We shuffled in and took seats in a huge circle of chairs pushed to the furthest ends of the room.

"Okay guys," Shai began, "I see you're tired so we're going to have an interesting discussion that will have you moving around the room."

Shai asked us to abandon our chairs and stand. There were some mumbles of dissatisfaction from the masses at his request. The metal-legged chairs squealed wildly as the forty of us pushed them back toward the blank walls and stood.

"Today we are going to discuss Israel's place among the world's Jewry and have a meaningful discussion based on some of these prompts and questions," Shai was reading monotone, directly from a placard provided by Taglit.

Taglit, named after the Hebrew word for "discover," is the parent organization that funds Birthright trips. Each year, nearly forty thousand qualifying Jewish young adults travel to Israel as a part of this program. Thirteen trip organizers, approved by Taglit Birthright Israel, organize and facilitate the trips out of North America. At roughly three thousand dollars a participant, their operating costs are over $300 million annually. When I was in

Israel, Taglit was celebrating its thirteenth year in operation. Everything that was being presented to us was cultivated and groomed by Taglit, its donors, and the Israeli government.

In 2011, Israel announced that it would donate $100 million to Taglit over a three-year period. This is a small amount compared to the $825 million that has been funneled back into Israel's economy since Birthright began in 2000. Needless to say, the State of Israel has a strong political and financial interest in the content presented by Birthright.

Shai continued to read in the same monotonous tone.

We all looked on without amusement and feeling more tired with every word he read.

"I'm going to read some statements about Israel and its relation to Jewish people in the world. After each statement, you can move around the room according to how strongly you agree or disagree. Let's say the wall to my left is Strongly Disagree and to my right is Strongly Agree. You can move anywhere between the two walls depending on your opinions. After the group is settled, we will discuss the statement," he rapped off from the paper he was holding.

I looked around the room to measure the general enthusiasm. Some of my trip mates were very content and eager to partake in the games and lectures. Some on the trip were there to mingle, drink when possible, and have a free vacation. Despite having a well-educated group, I was surprised to find how many of them lacked genuine curiosity in the topic of Israel in relation to world politics. It was during this game that the lines between Zionism and Judaism were blurred into one general topic, which was easily digested by most in our group.

Before we started the activity, Shai decided to stand on top of chair at the head of the room to situate himself above our shuffling. He stood statuesquely overhead and read the first statement.

"Israel should be the focal point of all world Jewry," he read plainly.

There were no sudden movements. Our group stood still for a moment to dissect the statement. I too, wasn't sure what I felt about it at first. I remained directly in the center of the room, where I stood originally while curious faces began skirting from one side to the other.

Shai looked down from his platform as the room quieted. I looked around to some of the people I was certain would speak first. There was eagerness in some eyes indicative of a listener just waiting for their turn to speak.

"Okay, so let's start with someone from the "Strongly Agree" side of the room," Shai said.

Without hesitation, a young man began to speak. We were all between twenty-two and twenty-six years old. I was highly interested in what he would say as I had personally witnessed him admit the day before that this trip was bringing him closer to his Jewish identity. He demonstrated this by purchasing a University of Michigan kippah from a vendor in Tzfat and wearing it proudly. I suspected it was mostly for the university affiliation.

"I think," he began with full confidence, "that Israel *IS* the focal point of world Jewry. I mean, this is our home."

He held back the deep visible emotion that was welling in his chest as he finished his sentence.

I did not know him well, but I had talked to him for a few minutes when we were all walking around the kibbutz. He was just out of medical school and was about to start a residency at a prestigious New England hospital. He mentioned that he was feeling very close to Israel since we had arrived. I listened intently to him then, but at that moment, I was seeing the full effects that this trip was having on him.

When we arrived, on our free trip, he was merely a boy who happened to be Jewish that was about to become a doctor. When he would return home, he would become an upper middle class Jew who supports Israel as the focal point of world Jewry.

It is important to remember that world Jewry and the state of Israel are not the same thing, and do not inherently share the same interests. Israel is a nation state with an international political agenda. Judaism is a religion. But this young man clearly was not aware that there was a separation. He made statements like, "this is our home," but when I asked him later he admitted that he would likely never move to Israel.

"Okay, let's hear from someone on the 'strongly disagree' side," Shai directed.

All eyes shifted from one side of the room to the other as another male voice rose from the crowd. It was Ben, my four-eyed friend from bus speed dating.

"So," he began creating an air of controversy, "Israel isn't the focal point. Statistically, there are more Jews in other parts of the world than in Israel, so it can't be the focal point," he said matter-of-factly.

Shai, still standing above us, began to interact with our mathematical arguer.

"If not Israel then where?" Shai asked with a hint of mockery.

"I don't know," Ben muttered, "maybe there shouldn't be a focal point at all."

This sentence caused quite a stir on the "agree" side of the room. Without hesitation, voices and hands shot out from the crowd.

Another male spoke up.

"It's obvious that there should be a focal point and it's clear that place should be Israel. This is the only place in the world that takes Jews in, no matter where we're from," argued one of our Ivy League educated group members.

My eyes shot over to him quickly as he made his case. I shook my head in disbelief. It had occurred to me that many people associate the state of Israel as a safe haven for Jews. However, I was in disbelief that such an educated person did not recognize that there were many Jews who had difficulty immigrating to the country, namely hundreds of thousands of Jews from Africa. Similarly, I recalled that before I left the United States for Israel I had a conversation with a woman who had celebrated that an African American Jew was finally received into another Israeli program after having to prove he was in fact Jewish. It is clear that Israel is not a home for all Jews. White American and European Jews are welcomed, even encouraged to move to Israel, while African and Black Jews face incredible discrimination.

Ben interjected, "I agree that Israel is a home to all Jews but to say that it should be the focal point of all Jewry doesn't make sense. New York City has as many Jews as Israel. Why not make that the focal point?" he asked in rebuttal.

New voices began to spring up in opposition.

"Because no one in New York cares about the Jews," said one voice.

"San Francisco has a lot of Jews too, maybe we should say that's the focal point?" argued another voice.

I looked around from face to face as arguments began to rise. I noticed that the only voices I was hearing were male.

Shai interjected from his throne and my eyes drifted up toward him,

"Okay okay," he said, trying to conduct the crowd, "what if we put numbers aside and just think about what it means to be Jewish. As a Jewish person, do you feel as if Israel is the focal point of Judaism?"

Everyone in the group had their heads inclined up to our guide as he delivered his question with a hushed voice of reason. I looked among the faces as they began to connect Judaism to Israel in their minds. A hand shot up from a guy in the center of the room. Shai nodded toward him and gave him the floor.

"Being Jewish, I always wanted to come to Israel, and now that I'm here, I feel more in touch with my heritage. We've stood in places that I've only read about in the Torah. It's obvious that this is the focal point for world Jewry."

He delivered his word with such sincerity that nearly every face that was twisted in opposition began to melt in agreement.

I raised my eyebrow in curiosity as I noticed the shift among my peers. The peace was quickly broken as Ben shouted more opposition.

Once again, I surveyed the room. I was sharing this space with thirty-eight young adults for whom Israel has been a state for their entire lives. Many of them had gone to Jewish schools and summer camps and had been taught about Israel's significance from a very young age. To most in the room, Israel and Judaism were never separate ideas. The few who had meandered over to the side of disagreement were only there because there are more Jews in other places in the world. I stood in the middle, watching shouts back and forth between Shai atop a chair, four-eyed Ben, and strong voices on the "agree" side. As tempers flared, it appeared as though we were entering into some serious posturing. Yet, it didn't feel as if anything was really being said. I was struggling to find a place to interject my own opinion, as the end of each sentence was an invitation for more argument. It was the perfect debate. Everything was said, nothing heard, and there were no resolutions.

"Okay guys," Shai nearly shouted over the opposing voices, "let's try another one."

Without much coercing, everyone fell quiet.

"Should Jews outside of Israel have a right to say what happens inside of Israel?"

Again, there was a quiet moment of contemplation before people began moving around the room. I looked on, mostly observing my peers. I decided to remain in the neutral zone of the room.

A few hands went up as people settled in their own place of agreement or disagreement. To my surprise, most of our group fell to the "disagree" side. I would have thought that a group so passionate about Israel would want to have a say in its policies.

Shai, still standing on the chair above us, gave the floor to our first woman speaker.

"I disagree that Jews outside of Israel should have a right to what happens within the country because they don't live here," she said.

It was a simple argument and most people standing next to her nodded in agreement.

Another voice rose up from a boy beside her in the crowd, "How would a Jew living in the U.S. be able to understand policy in Israel?"

There was more nodding.

"And how would we even be able to have a say? Could we vote online?" he asked curiously.

I looked on at the faces of those standing in agreement with our speakers. There was so many people on that one side of the room that if it were a boat, we would all be slipping to that one side. This image made think about group dynamics and the way deep political discussions like these can feel so overwhelming. I was personally overwhelmed and unable to articulate my ideas after the first statement had caused such a stir. Because of those feelings, I remained in the same spot in the room. I imagined that many others were overwhelmed by the intensity of some opinions and that instead of standing still like myself, they moved with the crowd.

I wanted to be a part of the conversation and I was feeling a strong desire to be involved, but before I knew it, our group had shifted from the original question to a new discussion about how we could use technology to become more involved in Israeli politics.

I was astonished at how fast the conversation was moving along. I wanted to go back to the last statement I heard.

"How would a Jew in the U.S. understand policy in Israel?"

More than half of our group was standing next to and agreeing with someone who basically said, the only way to be involved is to live in Israel, a point that would present itself again and again throughout our trip.

We would hear, often subliminally, "come to Israel. Live in Israel. There are programs to bring you back to Israel."

I wondered if anyone else felt these underlying messages, but the group had moved on to technological voting capabilities.

"You couldn't vote over the internet," shouted one voice.

"Cyber terrorism," shouted another.

What?! What are we even talking about? I wondered, annoyed.

These tangents, unfortunately, would become a theme for most of our group discussions.

Shai let the hypothetical internet voting discussion run on for far too long. I was longing to have a real discussion about Israel after several days of feeling as if there was no room for critical engagement or for me to speak up at all.

"Okay guys," Shai said, holding his hands up as a sign to stop. "Let's try another one."

I found myself becoming very frustrated. I wanted to talk more about the first two and suddenly we were on to a third. I shook my head in annoyance. As Shai looked through the statements for another one to share, I realized that he was taking a very precarious role in our conversation. Whether it was intentional or not, Shai, with a loud male voice, was choosing the other strong male voices to speak first. I noticed the desire to speak up on some of our female traveler's faces but, like myself, they could not find a way into the conversation. I had been through many heated group discussions such as this before. There is often a pattern of dominant male voices being heard over women. An experienced facilitator should make a point to silence majority voices and make room for minority voices to balance the discussion. Here this was not the case, and there is even more risk of exclusion when the facilitator is a man standing on chair waving his arms around, as Shai was doing.

I was feeling stifled for other reasons than the exclusively male dominated argument. We had been the audience of lecture after lecture since we had arrived in Israel. Each lecture or "discussion game" had only one side presented. Every word spoken during these presentations was making the case for Israel.

I would later find out that there is an entire job market in what is referred to as "Israel Advocacy," Shai being one of its star employees. Shai had been a tour guide for over twenty years and had been working with Taglit Birthright trips for most of their thirteen years of operation. This fact made me wonder how well he had crafted crowd control over his time as an advocate of Israel. I looked up at him, standing on the chair and wondered how many times he had facilitated this exact discussion before. He was in complete control of the discussion.

As the conversation of our third prompt began to derail, yet again, I began to feel strong agitation. I was in a strange and stifled position. Part of me wanted to speak out against the blatantly one-sided delivery of information to our group. The other part of me was muzzled and afraid that if I became a dissenting voice in any way I would be ostracized or kicked out of the trip. After all, I had signed a form in the airport that gave the right to the trip leaders to revoke my "gift" at any time, for any reason at all.

Even more frustrating was the flow of the conversation around the topics being introduced. It was repetitive. A statement was read, then a strong voice of agreement, a strong voice of opposition, and then a full on argument. This happened for each topic. I was feeling extremely uncomfortable. I distinctly remember having strong feelings of anxiety through the entire discussion. I wanted to speak up but my voice was not strong enough among the others. Those voices that were being heard, spoke with such urgency and conviction that it would fill even the most peaceful soul with distress.

Shouting fell furiously on my ears from each side of the room. I was overwhelmed, but soon the voices quieted. Shai began wrapping up with some trite words on how "complicated" the topics surrounding Israel are, which were illuminated by our "discussion."

I felt betrayed as I shook the feelings of anxiety from my body. The problem here was not that the topics at hand are inherently "complicated," but rather that the conversation we were having was full of people who weren't very well educated in them. We were a group of thirty-nine young adults, mostly told our whole lives that Israel was a homeland for Jews, but never having been told at what cost. Now, we were three days into being told over and over again about all the glory of Israel and no other stories or dissenting perspectives. No mention of Palestinian people at all. It would not have been hard to have a real discussion if we had more information.

Our group was dismissed until dinner and everyone had moved on to other topics. I moved along with the crowd out into the kibbutz courtyard. I felt the late afternoon sun as soon as we emerged from the building. My eyes flickered sleepily in its rays. I suddenly remembered how exhausted I was. When we were not physically running from place to place, we were being corralled into conversation mosh pits like the one we just exited. On top of that, I was still suffering from jetlag. We had a few hours until dinner. It took all my energy to get to my room and crawl into bed.

* * *

One of my roommates woke me for dinner and I shuffled groggily with her toward the dining room.

"Are you excited about tonight's lecture?" she asked.

"I didn't know we had another lecture. What's it about?" I wondered aloud.

"Israeli music history," she replied looking over anticipating I would match her enthusiasm.

"Huh, that could be cool," I responded with sincerity.

We walked the rest of the way without speaking. She found a friend waiting for her in the dining room, and I moved on toward a table with some other members of our group. I sat down to a discussion about Jell-O versus pudding. The things people talk about when they do not know each other is fascinating. I listened in, amused.

I was feeling hopeful about the music history lecture. I love music history and it felt like a nice break from one-sided political conversations. Even when we stood looking at a tree the previous day, Shai had tied it back into politics. I had heard an Israeli saying before I arrived, "Not everything in Israel is about politics. *Everything* in Israel is about politics."

It had been true so far, but a music history lecture sounded like pure entertainment.

I would soon find out the not-so-old adage would prove true, in spite of my hopes.

We were back in the same room we had found ourselves in countless times over the past three days. Again, the chairs were pushed as far back as the wall would allow. An attractive young Israeli woman stood at the front the room next to her laptop and a set of large speakers. I was impressed. It was a big setup for a seemingly small presentation. I was also relieved that our presenter was a woman, especially after that afternoon's lecture.

I took a seat in the front, right next to our presenter, and was beginning to feel excited.

As we all got settled, our presenter introduced herself. She spoke with an English accent as she explained she had been giving lectures such as this for many years. She mentioned she had graduated from a university in England having studied various countries' musical histories.

"Don't get too comfortable in those hard plastic chairs," she said jokingly. "We are going to do some moving."

She delivered her sentences humorously and swung her hips from left to right as she spoke. She smiled brightly as her skirt swayed under her movements. There was a lightness about her that was refreshing.

"Alright, let's get started," she said as she turned to her computer. She loaded an old grainy video clip that was filmed in one of the early kibbutzim.

I found it interesting where she started her history lesson. Israel was founded in 1948 while the kibbutzim were established as early as 1898. Her choice combined "Israeli" music history with Zionist music history, subtly implying that Israel had been around forever.

Before she played the clip, she gave a brief introduction to kibbutzim and their role in Israel.

"I guess by now everyone here knows what a kibbutz is?" she asked jokingly gesturing to our surroundings. "The people of the kibbutz started by living communally, sharing meals, growing food together, and celebrating with singing and dancing brought from the various countries they came from. They lived communally out of need, but when Israel won its independence, the kibbutz was able to transform. Today kibbutzim and members don't have to live communally to get by and have thriving businesses," she began.

With this one sentence, she had argued the validity Israel's statehood by suggesting it was only because of state power that people were able to rise out of their impoverished conditions.

I was skeptical of our lecturers since Shai's first hilltop speech. It was clear that topics and ideas presented to us were one-sided. This lecture was no different. Some may say I am too critical, but she chose her words intentionally and had delivered this message before. For a moment before the lecture began, I thought we might just have an evening of entertainment, but as she unfolded her presentation, the political agenda of the evening became clear.

She began clapping along with the first bit of music and encouraged us to all join along. The grainy clip exemplified an evening of dancing among the communards of a kibbutz. Everyone in the circle was beginning to loosen up by the second clip of similar substance.

"Are you guys too tired to try that dance we just saw?" she asked already motioning for us to stand up.

Before I knew it, we were all standing, holding hands, and moving counterclockwise. As we circled around all our faces lit up in smiles, including myself.

Our presenter played an old Russian Jewish song and taught us how to do the steps to the traditional dance. By the end of the song, we were all laughing uproariously and falling back into our chairs.

Mildly out of breath, our teacher continued with her lecture.

"Let's move on while we all catch our breath," she said smiling. "Does anyone here know about the army bands of Israel?" she asked.

No one seemed to. I was intrigued, though.

"Israel's music history is pretty bleak in its beginning years. In the 50s and 60s we, like most of the world, turned to the United States and Britain for our music. That is until the army bands of Israel started to move into the mainstream."

She played a selection of two catchy pop songs from the late fifties, hits produced by the official Israeli Army Band. I was more than a little astonished to learn that the Israel Defense Force was producing pop singles.

"For a while in Israel, there was no way to make it in the music scene unless you were in the army band. It was this band that produced some of the country's biggest artists."

As she played a third clip, I wondered deeply how that affected the early musicians of Israel. If it were necessary to go into the army to be a musician, how many people who subscribe to non-violence would be excluded?

How much music was missed because you had to be in the army band to be heard? Even more interesting is how clearly these examples showcased Israel as a militarist state.

She played the final clip from the military band and segued into the next decade. Before she began about the 70s in Israel music history she reflected on the military band.

"The music that came out of the army band transformed Israel's entire music history. It gave Israelis a place to share their talents and gave the country a feeling of unification, in addition to finally giving Israel its own musical identity. Everyone who is a citizen of this country has been through military service and it is this experience as individuals and as a nation that brings us closer together."

In a soft compelling voice, she was pitching army service as a bonding experience, for both those actively serving in the armed forces and in their lives as civilians.

Suddenly, as each person in our group was feeling kindred and bonding with Israeli history she said with passion, "There are many programs that pay for your transition to Israel. You all have a right to move here and become citizens."

I nearly burst out into a cry of "But, why?!"

I still could not wrap my head around the fact that we were on this free trip, experiencing Israel Advocacy at its pinnacle and being told of more ways to move here for free while millions of Palestinian refugees are still denied their basic Right of Return.

Our instructor continued on through the decades and introduced more music, genres, and styles. I enjoyed it for the most part, but while I had presumed the evening would be merely entertaining, it was as filled with propaganda as every other presentation I had attended on Birthright. I shook my head as we exited the building into the Israeli night. It was a mild late spring evening with the feel of a slowly approaching summer. The stars were vivid in the moonless sky and I was cooling down from the impromptu dubstep dance session that had finished her lecture.

It was a fun night, so fun that I almost forgot to be offended.

Chapter 6: Golan Heights and the Jordan River

The next day started off with an abruptness to which I was beginning to grow accustomed. We were up with the sun and eating breakfast between yawns. Soon, we were throwing our luggage in the bottom of the bus and ascending the coach staircase to the inception of another jam-packed day of activities.

Within minutes of pulling out of the kibbutz, Shai was in the microphone.

"Good morning," he offered his sleepy passengers. "Today is going to be a lot of fun, and we have a lot that we need to get done, so if you would be quick as we move through the day, then we can get to all of it," he instructed.

There were a few groans of opposition to his request for efficiency.

"Listen," he replied, "the quicker we get through all we have to do today the quicker we get to Tel-Aviv and you can have a night out in the city."

The previous groans had turned into howls of agreement.

We had all signed a waiver pledging we would not misuse alcohol, but it was an apparent theme among my travel mates that they were very excited to consume lots of alcohol at any possible time. We were officially in our fourth day and there had not been a night that was not concluded with a group of people hovering over a cheap bottle of vodka or wine.

It was becoming as clear as the vodka that most people on this trip were looking to mingle. Alcohol waivers aside, it was apparent that this trip was designed to accommodate a mingling crowd.

We had been through rounds and rounds of icebreakers to help us get to know each other, and there had been hints and suggestive language that we should be connecting more. We had even suffered through a few rounds of speed dating.

Shai put the microphone down and started flipping through his itinerary for the day. We had plans to hike the Golan Heights near Syria, raft down the Jordan River, and finish off our fourth day with a night out in Tel Aviv. He was thoroughly engrossed in his paperwork when Amy and Sara, giggling as usual, grabbed for the microphone.

I had heard them muttering to each other while Shai was talking, and I thought I heard Amy ask if anyone in the group had hooked up yet.

"Hey guys!," Sara quacked into the microphone. "So, we've got about thirty minutes until we get to the first part of our day and we were just talking about how you guys need to get to know each other better," she said with a wide smile.

Suddenly, I knew that I had heard her correctly. They were still wildly interested in assuring someone on this trip hooked up, even if they had to force it on us.

"We're going to do some bus interviews so you can *really* get to know each other," she informed us.

Shai glanced up at the girls briefly with a look of disapproval and quickly returned to his own agenda.

"Does anyone want to go first?" she asked tantalizing the crowd.

Without hesitation, one of the girls I had witnessed engrossed in several intimate conversations, shot out of her bus seat.

"I'll go!" she said making her way toward the front of the bus and shaking her long red hair as she shimmied through the aisle.

The night before, I had stumbled out of my room and into the grass, delirious with exhaustion and still trying to get over the jetlag. She had been sitting with one of the boys on our trip. They seemed to be "getting to know each other," fairly well, as Amy and Sara had hoped.

She bounced up to the microphone.

"Hey!" she offered cheerily to the crowd.

As much as I was not looking forward to hearing much about her, I was interested to hear what she might say. She was the perfect first interview for Sara and Amy, our secret matchmakers.

"Okay, let's start with your name," Sara said pushing the mic toward her mouth.

"Hey guys, my name is Kara," she said vibrantly.

"Hey Kara, thanks for being our first interview," Sara said.

She paused to think of another question.

"Oh, I have a good question for you. Are you a natural redhead?" she asked smirking.

Kara took the microphone and softly whispered, "I'm not."

"Oooo, so what's your natural color?" Amy implored.

"I'll never tell," Kara replied.

Everyone chuckled and there were even a couple of catcalls from the back of the bus. I felt like I was stuck in a mix of a Cosmopolitan article, an episode of Sex in the City, and a J-Date newsletter.

"Next question," Sara said, "Do you prefer American men or Israeli Men?"

This question got Shai's attention. With a look of fatherly concern, he glanced up from his task and continued to scowl at the girls in disapproval. Our Israeli guard suddenly became interested in the interview, as he was the only other Israeli man on the bus.

"Hmm, I think," Kara started slowly, "that it depends on the guy. It's not about where you're from, but more about who you are."

The bus filled with a big swooping "awwwweee" from the audience.

Blah. It was a little past 8:00 a.m. and I was being force fed yet another morning hookup game with Sara and Amy. I wanted to get my hands on their training manuals. I wondered if it was encouraged in their training that they play these roles. I was becoming less shocked by the hour of the design of the trip. Apparently, as this day would prove, it was completely acceptable to play matchmaker with the boys and girls and to shape the story of Israel's history in an extremely careful way to keep us from asking too many questions. After all, the biggest question we were to be asked on our trip was just about to be revealed by Sara.

"Okay, last question, and it's the most important," she paused, "Are you single and ready to mingle?"

The audience fell quiet as we waited for her response.

"Yes, I am," Kara said to an immediate applause.

"You heard it boys," Sara said provocatively into the microphone as Kara made her way to the back of the bus.

I sat looking out the window as we moved through the Israeli landscape. Sara and Amy settled into their seats laughing among themselves and getting ready for our day ahead. I watched the trees and green pass by my window and zoned out the bus chatter.

I was feeling marginalized. Whether or not I had read a book or two before the trip, and whether or not I was anticipating that there was a particular political slant to the trip I was a part of; I would have still felt as if I was personally being overshadowed. I would later find a small group of people within the group who shared my sentiments and would explain the trip design as "heteronormative."

Many group conversations and activities were working under the assumptions that everyone on this trip was heterosexual, monogamous, career driven, and working toward eventual procreation. Any other identities or lifestyle choices were far from being recognized or even acknowledged as existing. It was my own misfortune that I did not fall into any of those categories. We were on our way to Tel Aviv, one of the world's most "tolerant and open cities," and I had just felt a wave of anxiety come over me about my own sexual identity. I spent the remaining days of the trip avoiding the bus interviews so I wouldn't have to out myself, or even worse, lie to avoid judgment.

We pulled down a long gravel path that seemingly led to nowhere and came to a stop. Shai gave us some instructions before we unloaded.

"Guys, take water. If you don't have water, you can buy water from our bus driver. Make sure you're wearing sunscreen and you have a hat. It's going to get hot and this hike will take about three hours to complete, so make sure that you are in comfortable close-toed shoes."

It was information that Shai would give us again and again before the many hikes.

We finally descended into the warming morning and began another endless day.

Just like in Tzfat, we were alone for mere minutes before the swarms of other tour groups came chomping at our heels. Thirty minutes into our scenic canyon hike, our group of forty was interspersed with another large group that had a mind to move faster than we were. Suddenly, we were nearly one hundred people on hiking path that worked best if hiked single-file. The serene landscape was bustling with voices, laughter, complaining, and shouts of direction from each group's respective tour guide. It was a moment that would rear its head again and again: swarms of tourists all pushing their way through the Holy Land. We were only one hundred in two groups. At that same moment, maybe even a few hundred yards behind us, was another clusterfuck and another, and they spanned from the Golan Heights to the Red Sea.

Right after the most precarious part of the hike, where we hopped on stones in a rushing body of water, the massive group dissolved back into its smaller units. If the hike was meant to be majestic and peaceful, it was failing. I was finding that these day trips were, at most, helping me become more introverted from over-stimulation. In the days that followed, I would keep a distance from conversation clusters within the group and walk slowly in avoidance. It was seemingly impossible to be with my own thoughts.

Halfway through the hike, Shai slowed the pace and found a shaded spot for us to sit and relax for a few moments. We spread out, sitting on huge boulders and stretching from the intense terrain we had just hiked. A bottle of bug repellent circulated as we swatted mosquitos and flies from our skin.

The view was beautiful, the shade was friendly, and we sat in the quiet for a rare moment.

"This is the Golan Heights," Shai said, interrupting the stillness. He held his head up as the sunlight filtered through the tree's leaves and soaked his face.

"This part of Israel is one of the most beautiful in the country," he began. "It's a very fertile region that is important to agriculture in Israel. It's a large producer of mangoes and many other crops. It's also a part of Israel that we fought very hard to keep. Our neighbors didn't want us to have this land, but we stood strong and in what many refer to as a miracle we defended this land among giants"

He began to shuffle through his paperwork and took out a picture of Eli Cohen.

He told us the story of the Mossad spy who was captured during the six-day war and held in captivity by the Syrian government. The spy had infiltrated the Syrian army and was funneling secrets into Israel. These secrets would allow Israel to occupy and eventually annex the Golan Heights.

Syria refused to return the body of the spy, who died in captivity. Shai told us about a final letter he wrote his family before his execution. He began to read it to us, making sure to channel a patriotic spirit while reciting Cohen's final written words.

"He was killed in 1965 in Syria and his body has never returned to Israel, despite many attempts to retrieve it."

I sat, completely perplexed. What exactly was the moral of this story? To illustrate the merit of one of Israel's top spies? I found it hard to be enraged by Syria's refusal to return the body, as Shai's presentation suggested. I mean Cohen *was a spy* after all. Chelsea Manning surfaced in my mind immediately. A young American reveals state secrets in an effort to bring about transparency and is held captive without charges by her own country and against its own laws. That's something to be enraged about.

The story of Cohen the spy was topical. Syria continues to be an enemy of Israel, in fact, the two countries have never been at peace. Cohen represents an unfinished story. His body, never returned to his country, is used as a symbol of Syria's holdings that "belong" to Israel. The story victimizes Israel in a war that they won. Many stories told during Birthright would feature this same victimization.

We moved down through the canyon and into the last leg of the hike. It was nearly noon and we had been moving over rocks and pebbles, through creeks and mud, for almost three hours. As I shuffled toward the invisible finish line, another girl in our group caught my step and we were suddenly in a conversation.

"You're from New York, right?" she asked.

"Yeah," I responded, noticing her French accent. "And you, where are you from?" I wondered aloud.

"I am from France but I live in Brooklyn," she offered.

We talked about ourselves for a few minutes. I told her my interest in studying the structures and history of the kibbutzim movement.

"I think kibbutzim are awesome," she interjected, "all those people coming here to farm the land and make a new home," she said romantically.

"Um," I started to clarify, "I'm more interested in the anarchist governing models implemented in them and juxtaposing their original socialist anarcho-communist ideals with the forming of the State of Israel, or the way that those ideals were quickly lost as the state model took over."

She clearly didn't hear me and responded with, "Like how if it weren't for the kibbutzim there wouldn't be an Israel?"

"Um," I began again, "More like how it may be possible to have groups of self governing small communities without a larger government, or no state at all," I responded.

We didn't speak for a moment. I supposed she was digesting what I was interested in. I supposed incorrectly.

"Are you enjoying the trip?" she asked, completely off topic.

"Uhh, I wasn't really sure what to expect and I'm pretty tired."

It was all I could offer her.

I was longing to connect with someone with whom I shared some ideological similarities. There I was, in one of the most politically charged countries in the world, and we were all spending so much time listening and getting to know each other that we were not having any serious conversations. Surface conversations. Party conversations. Not real conversations.

During the last leg of our hike, the ground began to shake every so often and the sound of distant thunder would resonate through the open skies. I looked around to see if anyone was reacting to this apparent and close IDF bomb activity. Finally, someone asked Shai about it, to which he responded, "Don't worry, you're safe, it's just routine drills."

We finally spotted the bus and made our way from the three-hour nature hike to our next destination, the Syrian bunkers overlooking the Syrian border. It was from this lookout that we got a formal history of the Six Days War.

We unloaded the bus, once again, and walked up a pebbly path to the Syrian bunkers. Once again, other groups were moving among us. There was a group from Ohio, a group from Michigan, and multiple groups from Taglit. It would help to note here that the bunkers are not a vast and open space where hundreds of half interested young tourists fit comfortably. We were on top of each other, groups mixing with others, tour guides losing all their flock. It was chaotic with half the group either in the bathroom or buying coffee in the gift shop.

I noticed and found it very interesting that the tour guides, when they finally did get their groups back together, made a very specific point to be as

Hiking the Golan Heights during "routine" military explosions in the distance.

spread out as far as possible when they delivered their speech on the Six Day War. I would find out later from a man working in Israel Advocacy that this speech during the Birthright trip is regarded as one of the most important. The story of the Six Day War often makes Israel the David in a war against Goliath. Each tour guide has their own story of Israel's victory. Shai went on about the lack of equipment and the miracle of triumph. No matter the David versus Goliath story being told, it went unmentioned that Israel attacked preemptively, while the "giant" was sleeping and unprepared.

Israel admitted that the attacks on the Arab nations surrounding it were in fact pre-emptive. In the days that followed the Six Day War, leaders from nations around the world condemned the attack, stating they were in violation of the United Nations Charter.

It was only approaching 2:00 p.m. as we finished up lunch. I felt like I had traveled the world once over already and we were hardly through half of the day.

"Next stop, rafting the Jordan River," announced Shai, as we sped through the highways of northern Israel.

"We are slightly behind schedule because of all the other groups today. Depending on how long it takes you to get down the river will depend on how long you guys can stay out in Tel Aviv tonight," he said.

We unloaded, again, into another tourist-filled destination. I was noticing more with every stop how Israel was designed with tourism in mind. Every place we went had the feel of a theme park, complete with herds of school and church groups being shoved toward new attractions and lectures. This time, however, we were in for nothing more than a rafting trip. No speeches. We loaded into our rafts six at a time, were handed paddles and life jackets, and we were off. It was a small bit of autonomy that any adult would appreciate. It was a peaceful hour or so, rafting in such a beautiful place. If you could block out the noise of some of the younger groups of kids trying to bump and knock each other out of the rafts, then it was actually pretty serene.

Coincidentally, I was in a boat with Amy.

"If you had to be stuck in one television show for a week, what would it be?" I asked her from the boat's last row.

She turned around and smiled, "That's a great question," she paused. "I'm not sure, maybe *Family Guy*?"

We laughed. I expressed my interest in hearing better questions during the bus interviews. She agreed and asked me to write some and she would use them.

It was nearly 5:00 p.m. when we were at the other end of the rafting adventure and were waiting to board our bus again for the trip down to Tel Aviv. We all stood, slightly to completely soaked, as the hot afternoon sun begun to make its descent.

I was exhausted. Three hours of hiking, pushing through crowds, a dozen little conversations, too much listening and applying sunscreen. All I wanted to do when we boarded the bus was to sleep. Naturally, the first thing that happened was more bus interviews.

This time Sara and Amy interviewed one guy and one girl. The same big question at the end, "Are you single and ready to mingle?"

I was hardly listening when they wrapped up their interviews. My head was bouncing against the glass window as we sped south toward Tel Aviv.

I would begin writing questions after my nap. Unsurprisingly, they never did use them.

It was almost 8:00 p.m. when we finally arrived to the city. We had been racing the clock all day knowing that we had a midnight curfew set by Taglit.

"Okay guys," Shai began as those still napping began to stir. "We will be at the hotel in thirty minutes, and we can eat dinner right away and try to leave the hotel and get a couple of hours out tonight."

There was a shared excitement to be out in a vibrant metropolis and some clear annoyance that it was going to be so brief. Nearly everyone on the trip was from New York and looking forward to some time in a city after days of being in the woods and among the peaceful serenity of chattering tourists and open landscapes.

We rushed out of the bus and toward our hotel, shoveled hummus and falafel into our faces and went upstairs to make ourselves presentable after hours of being in the wilderness.

Slowly, thirty-nine young adults trickled out of the ocean-front hotel in Tel Aviv and congregated around the lobby doors. Most of the boys wore jeans and button downs, the girls in blouses and adorned in makeup and jewelry. It was a typical twenty-something outing, with the exception of our midnight curfew. It was approaching 10:00 p.m. as we finally boarded the bus to the part of the city where Birthright arranged to take almost all of its groups, Mike's Place.

Mike's Place is an Americanized bar sitting on the Mediterranean coastline. They cater to Israelis who want to hear American Top 40 and groups of American tourists who want to experience the same thing they do at home. Not my scene.

I was excited to have time away from the larger collective of our group. Throughout the long day I had managed to connect on a deeper level with a few of my trip mates. It was almost unspoken that we were not going to join the others at Mike's Place.

We all landed on the sidewalk as Shai barked orders on meeting back at this point by 12:15 a.m.. Thirty plus bodies headed straight toward the bar intended. I stood with what would become the counterculture collective of our Birthright group. I was later informed by some of my friends back home that this group naturally occurred in their experiences as well. The five of us would not have a serious conversation that evening, but these few people would save me from insanity on several occasions in the days following.

We walked slowly away from the madness that was unfolding behind us. It was Cinco de Mayo and there were two-for-one tequila shots at Mike's Place. The eager were crowned with sombreros and pulled inside.

I shuffled away with my new clique. We made our way toward a beach bar across the street and stumbled into a lazy hookah lounge. We all took a seat at a table closest to the water and spread our legs out into the sand beneath us.

It was one of the few minutes of serenity that I experienced on the trip. Ripe with exhaustion, we shared quiet and comical conversation over proper adult beverages. We gossiped about the others in our group as the water splashed near us.

"It feels as everyone here is trying to hook-up," Abe Said. "Even those in relationships."

Abe was engaged. There were a couple of people who were married and a couple in relationships, but as the trip unfolded, it became clear that some of those relationships at home were not considered sacred in the Holy Land.

"What about Sara and Amy?" Ben said with excitement. Ben was the nerdy guy I had told I would make people shit themselves for a superpower.

He was becoming a great person to share deeper conversations with, despite our first encounter being awkward.

"Do you guys think they are trained to be matchmakers or is that just the two of them?" I finally asked out loud.

"I know, right?!" Liora screeched.

Liora was the French Jew who I still wasn't sure understood my motivations as a human, but she made up for it by recognizing Sara and Amy as cupids.

"I wish the interviews were actually about getting to know people and less about trying to finding out who wants to fuck!" she exclaimed.

We all burst into laughter.

"I feel like I'm on a school trip," Ben started. "We're with a bunch of people we don't like who are either jocks, womanizers, or women weeding through the guys they like."

"We're in Tel Aviv, voted one of the most supposedly gay-friendly cities in the world, definitely in the Middle East, and we're not included in the conversation," I said.

Ben looked over at me as he realized he heard me out myself to our new crowd.

"You're totally right. All the conversations are super heteronormative," he admitted.

I was a little surprised that it was just occurring to him in this moment that this was a theme. If he, one of the more progressive thinkers in our group, wasn't seeing built in themes like this, how much were the others missing?

I wanted to bring up the fact that the maps they gave us did not show the boundaries of the West Bank and that we hadn't talked about Palestine yet, but I refrained. The trip gave me a sense of insecurity in many areas. I had no intention of being a voice of opposition on the trip; I only went on it to witness the program. Even so, it felt as if anything I brought up that was oppositional to the state of Israel could be seen as threatening and I felt uneasy about saying much of anything.

"I'm not surprised," Brian said, sitting forward a little in his chair.

"Israel wants as many Jews as possible to come live here and get married and have more Jewish babies. It makes sense that there's exclusion of homosexuals. After all, the state doesn't officially recognize marriages that aren't performed by a rabbi under very specific laws," he offered to the conversation.

"Yeah," I quickly jumped in, "The woman from the mikvah mentioned that! She said that it was also a requirement to go through three sessions at a mikvah before getting married in Israel. I thought it was a pretty solid business model," I quipped.

"Huh," Angelica started, "I didn't think about that before. It's so true though. There is a built-in guarantee that you'll sell a service if it's required by law."

Angelica was very quiet and had a perpetual look of boredom on her face. She was working in international affairs and foreign policy, a piece of information she kept quiet until the last day of the trip.

The waiter came back around and placed a huge hookah with blueberry tobacco right in the middle of our conversation. Its arrival shifted our discussion and we spent the remaining thirty or forty-five minutes of leisure time we were given enjoying the breeze and the ocean.

We settled our tab while laughing about our inability to understand dollar to shekel conversion without help from our waiter. We headed up the boardwalk and back across the street to our assigned meeting point only to find the mildly rowdy group we had left behind was now overflowing with tequila-infused belligerence.

At least twenty people were still missing from the group and Shai had gone into Mike's Place to find the rest of them.

I felt my voice quiet as the roar of the assembly got louder. Shai yelled for a count off.

"One."

"One."

"One!"

"Who is two?" Shai yelled into the laughing boisterous herd.

I was shocked at how differently my night had gone in comparison to the thirty others who had gone into Mike's Place. Everyone was wild with laughter and spirits. I looked on with my mouth slightly agape in wonder.

Shai yelled off for another count off. His request went unnoticed as another few stumbled out of the bar doors and into our group. Someone started singing a Backstreet Boys song, only to be joined by ten backup voices.

Frustrated, Shai pushed through the belligerent singing mass and counted each person himself. He herded us toward the open doors of our bus, counted again, and instructed the driver to take us to the hotel.

I sat in my normal seat in the front adjacent from our crew and Shai. He looked back at the drunkenness with extreme disapproval. I felt his frustration.

The singing did not stop from central Tel Aviv to the hotel. The Spice Girls, Celine Dion, and N'Sync sung acapella by thirty inebriated people.

We finally arrived back at the hotel. It was arranged that the hotel was nowhere near open bars or stores and the drinking was cut off immediately.

"We'll meet in the lobby tomorrow at 10 a.m.," Shai announced as groups huddled around the doors smoking and plotting to acquire more booze. "Tomorrow the soldiers will join us."

Eventually, the group dwindled down. Some admitting exhaustion and heading to bed, others changing and walking across the street to the beach. I sat quietly on a couch in the lobby with Ben and Brian. We seemed to be stuck on the couch, fixated on the behavior of the others in our group. It was complete chaos.

I was seconds away from excusing myself when I heard some yelling from outside the door. It was one of our intoxicated trip mates on the phone with his girlfriend back home.

"Whoa, that sounds rough," Ben joked, as he stood up.

It was pretty uncomfortable that we were within earshot. The guy was in between the sliding glass doors that led outside and the glass door to the lobby yelling at his girlfriend back in New Jersey.

"Don't be a dumb bitch," he slurred, "I'm on Birthright. It's not like I'm on vacation."

We looked at each other wide-eyed and silently excused ourselves from the scene.

Chapter 7: Mifgash Begins, Tel Aviv

It was our fifth morning, but it felt like the second or third week. Every moment in the previous four days had been spent together. Thirty-nine of us, moving around in small circles of conversation, sitting next to each other on the bus, or walking next to each other during hiking. I sought to spend a few minutes to myself, as I was still feeling pushed to my limits of socialization and activity.

I retreated to the lobby with my laptop to send emails and reconnect with the world that I lived in before Birthright began. As I was sitting on the same lobby couch as the previous night, I noticed Shai convening in another part of the lobby with the soldiers who would join our group later that morning.

It is expected on the Birthright trip that four or five soldiers join the group. Their presence is intended to give those on the trip a sense of what it's like to be an Israeli.

Shai was huddled closely with the six soldiers who would soon be integrated into our exhaustive daily schedule. I peeked at them over my laptop. Shai seemed to be giving them an orientation, although it was all in Hebrew, which I do not understand.

It was nearly time for us to convene and officially begin our day. Our group started to file downstairs from all directions. Shai, Amy and Sara corralled us all into a room connected to the lobby. We had become forty-five people with the addition of the six soldiers joining us. It was getting more and more difficult to find a comfortable way to arrange forty-five seats in any space, let alone get forty-five people to stop talking and start listening.

We formed a broken circle, with some left standing due to lack of chairs, and Shai began. He sat leaning over a pile of paperwork in his lap with a clean khaki colored kippah on his head.

"Good morning," he offered the still chattering crowd. "I hope everyone is feeling good after last night," he said sarcastically. "Today we are being joined by six soldiers for the remainder of our trip."

The six uniformed soldiers, two women and four men, were seated among our group and many eager voices had already started chatting with them.

"We're going to go around the circle and introduce ourselves really quickly. We are a big group so keep your introductions simple; name, where you're from and one thing about yourself."

We began yet another round of getting to know each other. Over the previous four days, we had been made to play countless icebreakers and name games. Learning thirty-eight people's names and things they may like was both frustrating and embarrassing. I mixed people up all the time, and now we were adding six more faces and names.

The round went fairly quickly and we were officially introduced.

"Okay guys," Shai said standing up, "We are going to get on the bus and head to the Tel-Aviv museum. Let's count off."

We were now forty-five after assigning the soldiers numbers.

The soldiers who are chosen to join Birthright groups are often in their final leg of service and speak very strong English. Among soldiers and Israelis the opportunity to join Birthright is known as a mifgash, and requires a sometimes intense application process. Israeli citizens who are attending university may also apply for mifgash. On my trip, only soldiers joined us, though our itinerary labeled them "peers." It is also rumored that soldiers/peers in relationships are often passed over for those who are single, and, I would assume, ready to mingle.

We loaded the bus and drove through Tel Aviv. Much like in Haifa, our bus driver expertly weaved through the narrow streets of one of Israel's biggest cities. He pulled over and we began unloading in front of Independence Hall. We were a few minutes early and had to kill time in the square in front of the hall. Naturally, groups were scheduled for specific time slots to ensure every Birthright and other youth Zionist groups were able to "experience Israel."

As we spread out in the plaza, Shai tried to keep us engaged by sharing some news about Tel Aviv.

"Real estate prices in Tel Aviv have been on the rise for the past few years. Earlier this year, a condo near this plaza sold for over nine million dollars," he informed those listening. "It's getting more and more popular to move to Tel Aviv and prices are skyrocketing. It's been great for the overall Israeli economy," he finished.

I stood facing Independence Hall with my hands in my pockets. It was humid and getting hotter as the morning got older. I squinted behind my sunglasses and observed the neighborhood. There were a couple of closed fine dining restaurants and a lot of development. Independence Hall was not very impressive architecturally, and there were cranes and scaffolding littering the skyline.

It was beginning to get crowded and people in our group were moving farther away from one another as we waited. I walked over to Brian, who was peering behind his Yankees cap and rubbing his blond beard contemplatively.

"Nine million for a condo," he declared. "Doesn't look like I could afford to live in Tel Aviv even if they wanted me to."

He smiled still holding his beard.

"Okay, guys! Let's go," Shai shouted toward us.

We began to file into Independence Hall. A group around our size was leaving the film screening room that we were about to enter. We waited, as was becoming expected, for dozens of people to file out before we filed in. I took a seat next to Angelica. I was finally beginning to shake the jetlag, but I was still exhausted from the previous night's activities. We nodded good morning as we settled in for the movie. A very vibrant man came quickly from the back of the room, adjusted the lights, and introduced the film.

"I am going to put on a movie about the history of Tel Aviv," he offered succinctly while pressing play on a hidden DVD player. He got up and moved quickly out of the room. As he closed the door I heard him give directions to the group that had just left. It was a busy morning for the hall.

We sat through the twenty-minute film outlining the history of Tel Aviv. Its most memorable parts were near the end, when it turned into the equivalent of a Carnival Cruise commercial from the 1980s. "Enjoy Tel Aviv!" a bright voice announced as a montage of happy couples and families from 1989 did just that.

The film finished before the urgent man who left us had reappeared. We sat in the dark for a few minutes, joking and speculating about the how old the film must have been. I enjoyed the darkness and the feeling of our loosened reins. It was a rare moment on the trip to not be led, pushed, or made to tell things about yourself.

Without warning, the fluorescent lights flashed on above us and nearly blinded me. I sat upright rubbing and trying to adjust my eyes.

"Sorry about the wait," said the same man in a hurried tone. "How was the movie?" he asked without waiting for responses. "It's great, I know. It's old, too. Yes, I've heard that before. I bet you'd all like me to leave the lights off and let you sleep, right?" he said chuckling.

He was seemingly scattered and perhaps on a high dosage of caffeine. He was entertaining, to himself at the very least.

"Okay, no, the lights are on now and I don't know how to turn them off anyways. It's harder than it looks like," he said in broken English.

He took a seat at the front of the room and started wildly searching for something under the desk beside him. Eventually, he pulled out a white binder and flung it open, flipping through its contents. When he found what he was looking for, he held it up for us to see, as though he was reading a children's book to us. He showed us a weathered print out of a film still that was stuffed in a plastic sheet protector.

"Okay, you saw this right, in the movie?" he asked without pausing. "It's Tel Aviv."

It was a picture of sand dunes. Nothing else.

"Yes, this was Tel Aviv. Just sand dunes. Nothing but sand, and sand, and sand, and then the ocean off in the distance with a bunch of salty water."

He flipped the page.

"Now this is Tel Aviv," he said holding up a more recent picture of the skyline of Tel Aviv.

Oddly, the first picture made it seem as if this land was completely barren and unoccupied. Only a few miles south of where we were sitting was the bustling city and port of Jaffa, one of the oldest ports in the world, and home to thousands of Palestinians before Zionist settlers pushed them out. The sand dune picture suggested that there was no one here before, which was simply not true. This sort of erasure of indigenous people is a common cultural tool of settler colonialism. Almost identical rhetoric has been employed in schools across North America for centuries.

Our host flipped through a couple more pages, showing them to us quickly and making awful jokes about the first mayor of Tel Aviv.

"Outside Independence Hall you can see a statue of Tel Aviv's first mayor on a horse, or a mare, and his name was Meir Dizengoff," he said laughing. "Mayor Meir, is that your mare?" he said laughing like a grandfather might after telling a bad joke.

He was strange and hyperactive and before we knew it, he was escorting us quickly to another room as the next group stood outside the doors waiting to go through the same process. Surely, he would tell the mayor joke again.

We moved into a large open room with seating on three sides. At the head of the room there was a raised platform where past leaders of the Zionist movement and Israeli state had sat. It was also the place where Ben Gurion, Israel's first prime minister, had read Israel's declaration of independence and announced its statehood in 1948.

I was revisiting a question that had been lingering with me since we arrived in Israel:

"Independence from who or what?"

I took a seat in the last row on the left side of the room. Several groups were coming in and taking seats. Another man who worked there began to make his way to the front of the room.

"Please take a seat. There are plenty of seats," he said to those still standing.

One of the soldiers sat next to me and smiled. I smiled back, nervously. I was unsure of how to break the ice with them. Though I was certain that was something that had already been planned into the agenda.

A new man now stood at a podium to the left of the raised stage. He took a microphone from the podium and began walking toward the front of the stage. Behind him were two long Israeli flags hugging a portrait of Theodore Herzl, the "father of Zionism."

"Thank you so much for coming to Independence Hall today," he began. "It is a pleasure to have young Jews from all over the world here with us in Israel."

There was an unexpected applause from around the room.

He continued, "In this very room where you are sitting, Israel became a state. Ben Gurion himself read this declaration in a live broadcast that we will listen to in just a few moments," he paused for a moment.

He spoke in segments and with a conviction that created a sense of importance around his words. He stood tall and proud in front of the huge Herzl portrait. All eyes were on this unnamed man.

"It was 4:00 p.m. Over two hundred people were crowded in this room to hear the declaration. Outside were hundreds more people listening to the broadcast. In just a few minutes, the state of Israel would become a reality for the Jewish people of the world."

He walked quietly to the side of the stage as an audio recording began playing over the loudspeakers of the hall. It was completely in Hebrew, but it was the original broadcast from 1948.

I had no idea what was being said in the recording and allowed myself to drift into other thoughts. I was watching the reactions on people's faces and wondered if they spoke enough Hebrew to know what was being said. I wasn't certain, but from the tone of Ben Gurion's voice I assumed the speech was coming to an end. On the other side of the room I spotted two young American girls holding onto each other's arms and crying passionately into each other's long hair. I looked at them perplexed. I didn't know what was being said, but even if they did I wondered what made it so emotive that it brought someone to tears. No one else seemed to be this moved.

The same nameless man came forth again and waited in brief silence.

"This is Eretz Israel. It is Israel. It is my home and it is yours. Welcome Home!" he shouted into the microphone just as *Hatikva*, the Israeli national anthem, began to play over the speaker system. I leaned back in my wooden chair as another startling round of applause began. Within moments it turned into a standing ovation. I half expected fireworks.

As we started to make our way out of the hall, I became engulfed in the crowd and unable to spot the weeping girls again, but I wanted to ask them why they were crying. It felt very staged—as if they were crying because it was expected, like at the end of *A Walk to Remember* or *Titanic*. It was something I would notice again and again. I even heard a few people speculate at what point in the trip they would likely cry.

As we walked out, I felt myself fill with many questions that I wanted to ask, but a feeling of dread draped around them. I could not find the words to ask, "Independence from what?" to our Israeli-born tour guide, and there was no room for questions in the hall.

I was particularly frustrated because it was a legitimate and earnest question, but I worried I would come off as offensive if I asked. It seemed to me that there was a misunderstanding, or even a misuse, of the word "independence."

In the Declaration of Independence of the United States of America, a document with which my educated group mates and I were familiar, there was a clear goal of independence from Britain. In Israel's case, there was not so much a declaration of independence as much as it was a declaration of statehood. The boundaries of what was to become Israel were already carved out by the United Nations. There was no need for an "Independence War" or a "Declaration of Independence," as it is popularly understood in American terms. If anything, it was a war of the expulsion of the Palestinians. However, the language, or the translation, suggested otherwise. It was a question I felt was too controversial to resolve publicly during the trip.

We were pushed back across the street and into the square where we had been dropped off. I slipped my sunglasses back on and looked around. I spotted the horse statue and chuckled to myself knowing that the hyperactive man was going on about it all day long. It was nearly lunchtime, often the only time during the day when we had some autonomy.

"Okay guys, let's count off," Shai shouted at us.

We struggled through the count, with our Israeli soldiers having pronunciation troubles. Forty-four is apparently a tricky number to say when your first language is Hebrew.

"We're going to get back on the bus and go to Allenbi Street and market for lunch. We'll give you about an hour or so to eat and look around Tel Aviv and then we need to get back on the bus and head south. We have a long day ahead of us tomorrow so it's going to be an early night," Shai informed us all.

I was excited to have some time out in a metropolis after several days in the seclusion of the kibbutz. We unloaded on the busy streets of central Tel Aviv, and groups of people started going in different directions. I began walking with my own group, but veered off onto my own path not long after we started. I left them unannounced and began down a different street than anyone else in my group. If nothing else, this would be a good time to be in my own thoughts after so many days of nonstop talking.

I walked around, taking note of how Americanized the stores were. Shirts with Mickey Mouse and Winnie-the-Pooh lined the windows of one storefront. I wanted to find a bookstore, sit, have coffee, write about life, etc. Unfortunately, I could not find that type of place in the short amount of time we had. I spent the majority of my free/runaway time trying to find my way back to the pickup location. The time flew by and before I knew it:

"One."

"Two."

And so on.

We loaded the bus and began toward our next destination, Arad.

On the way out of the city, we stopped briefly and unloaded into Rabin Square. Shai walked us quickly through the square named after Israel's only assassinated Prime Minister. As we walked, Shai told of Rabin's dedication to the peace process. We stopped and gathered around Shai as he stopped walking.

"Just over there," he said pointing behind him, "is where Rabin was assassinated. An oppositional group that didn't agree with his plans for peace killed him. He was one of Israel's top peace advocates and struggled throughout his life to bring the two sides together."

As Shai paused for a moment to clear his throat, an older woman approached our group and began shouting at us in Hebrew. She had apparently been standing and listening the whole time while Shai spoke of Rabin. In our group, only one person spoke Hebrew fluently so what the old woman said went mostly unrecognized, though she was very animated about it.

I found out later that she was saying it was a terrorist attack by an extremist right wing Zionist group who did not believe that Palestinians had any rights to the land they occupied, and Rabin was in favor of a two-state solution. She was trying to explain that if Israeli citizens could not get along, then there was no hope for a peace process. Shai, for whatever reasons, did not translate her during her rant or mention that an Israeli right wing extremist killed Rabin. Instead, he kept calm when speaking to her and began walking us toward the bus that was waiting for us on the other side of the square. I only found out what she said later by asking the one guy who spoke Hebrew in our group. I still didn't feel close enough to our Israeli soldiers to ask them. I was beginning to notice that Shai was very settled in the way he gave his tours, and he would keep information from us to keep us from reacting. In this instance it was to keep us from starting a political discussion, but he would do it with many other things as well.

We boarded the bus and headed toward Arad, a small town near the western edge of Israel. When we arrived, there was nothing to be seen except desert and our hotel for the evening, which was the same color as the sand beyond it. It was an unsightly small town with a few buildings and a lot of wind. We unloaded, got settled in our rooms, and headed back down for dinner.

During our meal, Shai got up and announced that we would have an activity in the conference room downstairs right after dinner. There was some grumbling about the endless after-dinner activities. We all longed for a slow night where we got to do whatever we wanted, even if there was nothing to do in the town we were in. Nonetheless, we hurried through another meal of hummus and schnitzel and headed down to the conference room where we played another ice-breaker game with the soldiers.

As we finished up our nightly activity, Shai began telling us of the next day's agenda in a serious voice.

"As you already know, there are two nights that you can't have alcohol. Tonight is one of those nights. Tomorrow we will climb Masada, an ancient fortress, and we will start very early."

There were moans of dissatisfaction from most of the group. We were halfway through the trip, and whatever earlier motivations people had for being polite were waning. I grunted as well. We had started so many mornings early I was getting accustomed to the early morning routine.

"Tomorrow morning we will leave here and bus to Masada and climb in time to watch the sunrise over the Dead Sea. It's very important that we leave on time so that we don't miss the sunrise and so that we don't get caught in a bunch of other groups who are going to Masada as well," he said matter-of-factly.

There was a silence as we waited to hear what time we had to be up. I could see concern on my peers' faces as they tried to figure out what time sunrise was. I too was wondering.

"We'll leave here tomorrow morning at 4:30 a.m." Shai announced finally. "Be sure to get a lot of sleep. Tomorrow is going to be a long day."

Chapter 8: Exhaustion at Masada and the Dead Sea

I awoke at 4:15 a.m. to the other girls in my dorm room starting to stir. We had fifteen minutes to get dressed, pack, and get onto the bus. The morning started in nearly complete silence, nothing but the sounds of zipping and rolling luggage.

The sky was midnight black and littered with stars as we walked out into the cold desert air and began loading the bus. We pulled away from our lonely hotel and plunged forward into the darkness.

There was no light pollution from the small town of Arad and as soon as we were a few hundred feet away, our bus was surrounded by sand and dark. The headlights of the bus lit the barren desert as we swerved through its landscape.

Shai gently began speaking into the mic.

"Boker tov, and good morning," he nearly whispered. "Sunrise is in a little less than one hour, and it should take us around thirty minutes to hike to the top of Masada. We have plenty of time," he said assuredly, "but, there are going to be a lot of groups that are making the same hike, so you'll want to move quickly so that we don't miss the sunrise," he finished factually.

We drove further into the desert along narrow winding roads before finally coming to a big parking lot at the base of the Masada. We were one of the first charter buses in the lot, but as we unloaded, one after another began to pull up. There was some last minute shuffling after we were off the bus. A group went to the bathroom and I followed so I could put in my contacts, which I did not have time to do before we left.

I peered through my glasses and the darkness at the ancient fortress we were here to see. Masada was built around 30 B.C.E. and was fully excavated in the 1960s. Similar to Machu Picchu, Masada is a stone fortress on the top of a mountain—and one that I did not look forward to climbing before dawn.

We gathered around Shai, performed a quick count off and began our ascent into what would soon become one of the longest days of my life.

The hike up was mild, at first, but became steeper the longer we walked. It was just after 5:00 a.m. and the black sky was beginning to break with color from the approaching sunrise. We were together to begin with, but as the hike became harder scores of kids and teens as well as other groups scattered between us, everyone weaving toward the top. In hindsight, it was an easy hike, but at 5:00 a.m. with hordes of chattering teens and screaming youth, it felt impossible. There was a handrail near the top where the climb became steeper. I found myself clenching onto it mostly out of internal fatigue and less out of physical need for support. There was a push from behind as dozens of people, fearing they would miss the sunrise, began to run up the path, and suddenly, we were at the top. The sun was still below the horizon but its rays were menacingly piercing the skyline.

The endless groups began to find their own viewpoints and cluster around the wall facing east. Below us was a picturesque view of the Dead Sea, covered in a blurred morning haze. Our group of forty-five people huddled into an enclave of the ancient mountaintop ruins and waited for the sunrise.

Behind us, Shai found a secluded spot to himself and began his morning prayers. He covered himself in Tallit, a prayer shawl, and began wrapping his arm and head in Tefillin. Sara and Amy excitedly corralled us into taking a quick picture before the sunrise, and then we waited. Everyone stared over the edge toward the horizon and waited to be the first to see the sun break.

Finally, the fiery golden sphere peeked from behind the curtains of the Dead Sea. There were a few sets of hands that found the daily phenomenon worthy of applause, and a lot of endearing "ooos" and "awws." It was beautiful to watch the sky break from deep reds and purples to grapefruit pinks and orange hues, but only seconds after the three or four minutes it took for the sun to completely come over the horizon below us, I remembered how absolutely tired I was.

It was still before 6:00 a.m. and we had already hiked to the top of an ancient fortress and watched the sunrise over one of the most well known bodies of water in the world. I felt that there was much reason to be feeling exhausted, and it was setting in on me hard. I began yawning frequently and trying to shake the sleep from my body.

We gathered in groups, talking and chatting while Shai finished his prayers. I wasn't sure what we were supposed to be doing for the rest of the day, but I assumed it would include breakfast. Some people in our group had an itinerary that they printed out from online before we departed, but since we had been in Israel, Shai kept us mostly in the dark of coming activities and at times changed the itinerary. After twenty years of being a group tour guide, Shai had learned a lot about crowd control and group dynamics. Often, he would fail to mention uncomfortable facts or make changes so seamlessly that I didn't know what was coming until we were doing it.

The sun had been up for about a half an hour when Shai had us gathering around him. He began talking about the place we were standing, Masada, and its history. I felt my body begin to warm up in the desert sun and I felt even more tired than before. I slid to the back of the pack and leaned against a wall trying to remain awake as Shai continued his presentation.

We walked from viewpoint to viewpoint on the mountain top ruins, as the sun grew hotter and hotter. I noticed a few others in my group having a hard time keeping their eyes open as well. I was wearing a hoodie and jeans, which seemed appropriate when we unloaded the bus in the dark of the brisk desert morning, but, as the sun climbed, I was increasingly uncomfortable and tired.

Eventually, Shai concluded his speech.

"Okay guys, we are going to walk down the Snake Path and then have breakfast. It should take about thirty to forty-five minutes to get to the bottom."

The group let out a groan of dismay in unison. We had been up since 4:00 a.m. and walking around some old dusty ruins that were now baking in the desert sun, and all before breakfast. Disapproval aside, we began our descent. I was holding my hoodie as we began to walk down the nine-hundred plus stairs. Walking down stairs seems easier than walking up, until you do it. Ten minutes into the descent, my calves began to cramp. Fifteen minutes into the walk down, I ran out of water. The sun was hotter with every step.

Within the walls of Masada after sunrise.

Snake trail. Nine-hundred plus steps to exit Masada Fortress.

Twenty minutes into it, I began to lose all my pride and starting slowing down so much that most of my group was either very far ahead or screaming behind me out of the fear of heights. There was a railing that ran down the path, and two or three people in our group were clutching onto it for dear life as they walked down. The steps were wide and short, which made it slightly more tolerable. I was out of water, in jeans, under the desert sun, and my calves were cramping beyond belief.

Thirty minutes into the descent, I began to get stiffness in my neck and my eyes were losing their ability to focus. I wasn't sweating but I was very hot. I had rolled my jeans up to my knees long before but was still overheated. I silently blamed Shai for my fatigue. He never mentioned we would descend nine-hundred plus stairs in the mid morning sun and that it was so physically exhaustive we might feel like passing out.

As I reached the bottom, without water and my calf muscles burning, I found myself incredibly delirious and tight in my neck. A few people from my group rushed toward me as I tried to get my footing and swayed toward fainting. I managed to not faint, and even to walk myself to a seat near the entrance of the gift shop. I rehydrated as we waited for the entire group to gather.

"You okay?" Ben asked with concern.

I sighed heavily and nodded, though I felt the effects of heat exhaustion.

We counted off and headed inside the air-conditioned cafeteria toward breakfast, finally. It was just past 9:00 a.m.

I went toward the water and filled cup after cup until I began to feel hydrated. We ate in the crowded, bustling cafeteria from a buffet and clumped into conversation circles. We were given over an hour to eat and reassemble. With nothing else to do after eating, we all ended up in the enormous gift shop. If Israel had a product, it was being sold in the Masada gift shop. Dead Sea salt scrubs, wine from the Golan Heights, boxer-shorts with the Israeli flag, and the flip-flops to match were all available for purchase.

I meandered through the departments in awe of how much commercialization had managed to find its way onto the ancient mountaintop fortress.

I was still recovering from my close call with heat exhaustion. I found a bench near the entrance of the food court/cafeteria/gift shop and waited for the next part of this already exhausting day to unfold.

It had been spoken several times already that it was unacceptable to opt out of activities. Part of the agreement of the Birthright "gift" is that the participant must participate in all of the activities, or they may be in danger of having their "gift" revoked. The consequences of this revocation could potentially include repaying of the "gift," and being asked to leave the trip. With the current value the "gift" valued at three-thousand dollars, that meant, no matter how exhausted or offended I found myself, I continued on.

It was around 10:30 a.m. and we were back on the bus headed toward Ein Gedi, a nature reserve with several beautiful waterfalls, for a "nature walk."

Before disembarking the bus, Shai stood to give an announcement.

"Listen guys," he said getting our attention. "This is not that much of a hike and more of a nature walk so there's no need to get changed out of the clothes you are already wearing. It's very important, however, that you bring a lot of water and wear something on your head." He let out a heavy sigh. "This time, no one will be let off the bus without water and a hat or head covering. These are Taglit rules and it's especially important on this activity because someone from the Taglit Birthright offices will be here to critique my group," he finished, obviously annoyed with the bureaucracy.

We unloaded under the cloudless sky and I began to drink my water before we ever left the parking area. As my eyes adjusted to the blazing sun, I noticed the masses of groups all around us. Everywhere we went, there were hundreds before us and after us. We were only a small fraction of the massive guided group tourism industry of Israel.

The easy walk felt more like an intermediate hike. There was both an incline and a jagged path ahead of us and, without fail, we found ourselves in a never-ending line of other tour groups. The paths were made for single-filed hikers. I looked up toward the top of the trails to find an endless line of bodies marching slowly on toward viewpoints and waterfall holes. It was the equivalent of waiting in line at a theme park under the blazing hot sun with teens and sweaty, grumpy adults, all groaning about the seemingly infinite wait.

Less than thirty minutes into the adventure, I was furiously overheated and nearly out of water. I regretted not changing out of the jeans I had worn on the previous hike. We moved slowly up the reserve, with Shai occasionally attempting, and failing, to tell us about our surroundings. The hike was too crowded for educational pit stops. Every time we stopped, hordes of pushing people from behind us would rush angrily past. All age groups were present, including Israeli school groups and U.S. senior citizens.

Suddenly, I found myself beside one of the female soldiers.

"How are you enjoying this?" I asked sarcastically motioning to the constant line of bodies.

"It's okay," she responded in a soft Israeli accent.

"Have you been here before?" I asked.

"Yes," she replied, "more than once."

"Oh," I said with shock. "How about Masada?"

"Yeah, I've been there too," she said smiling and pointing to her t-shirt. It read, "Been there. Done that."

"Ha!" I exclaimed. "Good t-shirt to wear today."

We got separated not long after our short exchange, but it stuck with me as we walked on. Each of the soldiers joining us had likely been to all of the places we had visited before. There was nothing new for them to see on these adventures. I realized this at about the same time that I noticed the way a couple of the male soldiers were interacting in our group.

"Hi," one of them said as he paced himself with me and began to walk closer.

"Hey," I responded, slightly startled.

He had on super-short aquamarine shorts that showed off his olive-skinned-military-conditioned legs.

"It's beautiful out here, isn't it?" he asked.

"It could be," I responded.

"How?" he asked genuinely curious.

"If there weren't hundreds of other people here, then it could be really magical," I answered.

He paused.

"So," I said finally, "what part of the military are you in?"

"I'm the one who shoots the rockets out of the sky," he replied with pride.

"Oh. Interesting, I heard about that," I said with intrigue. "Does that happen often?"

"Not really," he replied.

The conversation faded and I noticed him drift from me to another girl in our group. I did not feel too bad to lose the company as most of my thoughts were around how incredibly uncomfortable I was under the burning sun. I was out of water. We had seen two waterfalls that were quite small and were still among far too many people. It was decided by Shai that we would descend instead of trying to push through the crowds to another waterfall. We made our way down quickly and I found the nearest water fountain and began to rehydrate again.

It was early afternoon when we got back on the bus and headed toward our next stop: the Dead Sea. I have to admit that among all the things we would do on this trip, the Dead Sea was one I was looking forward to in particular. However, my enthusiasm was minimal as we approached a parking lot attached to an "activity center" on the shore of the sea.

"Okay guys," Shai began in the microphone, "It's a little after 1:00 p.m.. Let's meet back up around 3:30. That should give you plenty of time. There are bathrooms inside for you to change and there are showers as well. I think you can buy a bucket of mud that has healing properties in it. I'm not too sure how much it costs, but someone at the desk can help you. There is also a food court, so bring money for lunch," he finished.

I do not know what I was expecting, but I knew that another tourist center with a gift shop was not it. I looked through the window of the bus at the commercial building on the mouth of the Dead Sea. I was filled with disenchantment and began to pack my laptop along with my bathing suit. I wasn't sure if I wanted to go into the water, between being up since 4:00 a.m. and the massive disappointment of finding the sea so highly commercialized for tourism. I brought my computer to answer some emails that I hadn't had the time to read since we arrived.

More than half of our group began a mad dash toward the changing rooms when we entered into the air-conditioned gift shop. I meandered toward the food court downstairs that was overlooking the resort-like setup on the beach. Lounge chairs and umbrellas littered the sand and groups of bobbing heads were already out in the water. It was quiet in the dining area where I found a seat alone and began to process some of the long day.

It was 2:00 p.m. and I had watched the sunrise on an ancient fortress, walked down over nine hundred stairs, and descended into near heat exhaustion. I had walked single file up the sometimes-steep nature reserve of

Ein Gedi, and now I sat staring out of panoramic windows at the Dead Sea —and all before lunch. If I wasn't as affected by the commercialization of this destination, I would have already been in the water with everyone else. It was in this moment alone that I had the opportunity to wrap my head around some underlying themes in our itinerary that day. We were only forty Americans among thousands that attend Taglit Birthright every year. These trips were hugely impactful for the tourism industry of Israel. We never paid an entrance fee at any place we went, but it was certain that just because we did not wait in line, did not mean that it wasn't being paid. The entrance fee to Ein Gedi is approximately seven U.S. dollars per person. The entrance fee to Masada for groups of more than thirty is approximately six U.S. dollars, and it surely wasn't free to enter our private Dead Sea oasis center.

The estimated cost per Birthright participant is three-thousand dollars. The airfare can comfortably eat half of that cost, which goes back into Israel's national airline that you may remember is still partly owned by the state. Some of the remaining funds go toward entrance fees at endless destinations further fueling Israel's economy.

I sat staring at my group out the window, playfully petting each other with handfuls of wet mud. I closed my laptop and went to change into my bathing suit. Despite my exhaustion and criticism of the oasis center, there was no way I could be at the Dead Sea and not go in.

Chapter 9: A Night at a Bedouin "Camp"

We were pulling away from our Dead Sea oasis and headed toward our final stop of the day, the Bedouin tents. This was the activity that promised a camel ride and a new epic Facebook profile picture.

I was putting a salt rock from the sea carefully into my bag when Ben sat down beside me.

"Hey, wasn't that cool?" he asked nodding his head excitedly.

"Yeah, it was really surreal," I answered.

Everyone was suddenly lively with chatter after the gravity-defying experience we had all just shared. It had been so much fun that it temporarily broke down my sullen disposition.

I talked wildly with Ben and a few others about how intense the physical experience of the Dead Sea was as we drove quickly toward a nearby Bedouin camp.

I didn't know much, if anything, about the Bedouin culture, but as soon as we pulled into the "camp" I got the sense that this was more of a tourist attraction than anything else.

We exited the bus at around 4:30 p.m. The sunset was in less than an hour and we still had more items on the agenda for the day. Nearly twelve hours of nonstop activity led into more as we were quickly ushered from the bus to an open tent. I noticed Shai talking with some workers at the camp and arranging our slot to ride the camels. We were only one group among many that were in the camp that night, and we had to wait our turn to ride the seemingly tired camels.

Behind the camp, in the open desert, were around twenty-five camels, all tied together in a line, with dry mouths and big sad empty eyes. They were loading up another group and the "camel ride" employees were helping kids onto the backs of the kneeling giants. I was reminded of a theme park again when I noticed all the employees of the camp wore bright blue t-shirts, except, of course, the Bedouins. Two or three dark skinned Bedouin men helped with the camels and walked quietly beside the tour as they took off.

On the other side of the camp, we entered the open tent and were asked to sit down on the rugs laid out over the dirt floor. At the head of the tent was a Bedouin man. He waited patiently for us to enter and sit down. Shai greeted him warmly as we got settled, then introduced him to us.

"Salem is a Bedouin here in the desert of Israel. His people have lived here, mostly nomadically, for centuries. He is going to share some of his culture with you."

Shai took a seat near me in the front and looked on intently.

Salem introduced himself as trays filled with tiny ceramic cups of cold coffee were passed among us. He explained that it was customary to give coffee to guests when they entered a Bedouin home. He was playful and light hearted. His accent made it hard to understand everything he said, but I could tell that it was a speech he gave many times before and would likely give many more times that evening. I did not doubt that he was Bedouin, but there was something eerie about our theme park surroundings that took away from his presentation.

He shared some music, jokes, and stories with us and without segue announced that he was expecting another group and that we must be going. And so it was.

Shai thanked him again as we all headed out of the tent and toward our next attraction, the camels.

As we exited the tent, I noticed quite a few scrutinizing faces. So far on our trip, the disingenuous nature of many stops had been well cloaked. However, it was apparent that this camp was nothing more than a tourist attraction. It lacked the sincerity of many places we had been, and, suddenly, this scrutiny was percolating in other minds than just my own.

We climbed on top of our tired and saddled desert creatures just in time to catch the sunset over the desert horizon. It was a beautiful landscape, despite the ill nature of the overworked camels. A couple of Bedouin men walked with us through the sands and guided our tour. Pictures were taken, screams were had, and the sun set right as we made it back to camp. The fatigued camels kneeled in the sand at the demands of their wranglers and we hopped off gleefully and headed back toward the camp.

Shai met us and began leading us to where we would be sleeping that night. We entered a huge open tent with a divider in the doorway. Another Birthright group from California was on the other side of the makeshift wall and were talking and joking loudly as we entered.

Our sleep arrangements for the evening were a huge empty floor, flimsy foam mattresses, and dusty pillows. I fetched a mattress and took it to the furthest corner of the tent. As I made my bed, I noticed pieces of sand and dirt floating among the light particles like desert confetti.

My newly founded group of like-minded friends joined me in the corner. It was apparent that there were some flirtations between a few guys and girls and it was almost guaranteed that after nights of gender separation this would be the ideal setting for some heavy petting. In the opposing corner of the tent, we spotted a female soldier nuzzling the guy who had been yelling at his girlfriend on the phone a few nights before.

I was exhausted and lying prostrate on my mattress. I had a feeling as if I could fall asleep forever, but it was interrupted by an announcement that it was dinnertime.

I dragged my tired corpse to the dinner tent, where I, still with my clique, took a seat on the ground and awaited the blue shirts to bring the food. Shai, having nowhere else to sit, joined our table.

As we joked around in our shared deliriousness, our food arrived. We ate, mostly with our hands, and furiously, like we had been up since before the sunrise.

Our dinner conversation was mostly light, until Shai eagerly asked, “What did you think of Salem and Bedouin culture?”

Earlier I watched Shai greet Salem warmly, as if he were an old friend. Having noticed this earlier, I didn’t answer at first.

“I think,” Ben started slowly, “that it’s kind of sad,” he finished.

Shai looked shocked and puzzled.

“What?” he scoffed in reply.

“I can see what you mean,” I spoke up quickly in Ben’s defense.

Shai looked stumped. Genuinely stumped.

Ben and I exchanged quick glances as we realized Shai was not taking this opinion well.

"How is it sad?" Shai asked, semi-annoyed.

"It's just that," Ben started sympathetically, "it seems like the Bedouin people have a rich history, but that it's not the same as it once was. Like Salem said, they aren't really nomadic anymore. There's a lot that has changed," he answered hurriedly.

"I get what you mean," Brian said. "It doesn't seem like there is a lot of Bedouin culture left in Israel," he finished.

Shai looked at us in disbelief, "What do you mean there's no Bedouin culture? Salem is Bedouin. His family and his stories are Bedouin," he replied.

"Shai," I started with empathy, "there may still be a Bedouin culture in Israel but what we're saying is that *this* is not Bedouin culture."

"Whatever," he replied laughing.

He used the word "whatever" quite often. It was kind of cute to hear a middle-aged Israeli man sound like a teenage American girl, and the comedy of it made the mood much lighter. We quickly shifted topics and waited to express our feelings until he excused himself from the table.

We all remained seated along the floor as the camp's staff cleared our tables. Shai had started mingling with some of the other tour guides, none of whom would be sleeping in the dirt filled tent hotels we were provided with.

My group sat in lethargy. We were satiated with Bedouin cuisine and unraveling after such a long day. Slowly, we got more and more comfortable on the cushions beneath us until we were mostly lying down.

"What about Shai?" Ben asked after he was finally out of earshot.

"Yeah, that conversation felt weird. He can't really believe that this place is genuine and a true representation of Bedouin culture," I said assuredly. "Or maybe he does." I retracted sadly in my next breath.

In the decades since Israel declared statehood, Bedouin culture has greatly changed. They are becoming less and less nomadic people and have started building stationery homes in the desert. These structures are often built without oversight or permits and some have been ordered by the state of Israel to be abandoned or dismantled. These "unrecognized villages," as referred to by Israel, are home to nearly one hundred thousand Bedouin people. As a result of being "unrecognized," they are denied state services, such as water and power. Where we were staying had many showers and plenty of power, and issues of "unrecognized villages" went unmentioned.

As it turns out, the camp we were staying at was founded in 1999, the same year as the Birthright trip.

Eventually, the crowd began to move out of the dining tent and into the vast endless desert night. There was a lot of light pollution from the camp, so the previous promise of a vivid starry sky went unfulfilled. There must have been more than ten groups as large as ours mingling throughout the camp. There were Birthright groups around our age as well as many other American Jewish youth groups that were much younger. Hordes of people rushed from tent to tent, giggling wildly. It seemed as if all the chaperones were suddenly missing. Shai had wandered off with a group of other tour guides earlier in the evening, and our matchmakers were lost in the shuffling crowd.

I sat on a low sitting bench with a few people from our group and chatted for a bit in the desert night.

"So, this is a weird place," said one of my travel companions. "I heard it's funded by Jewish-American philanthropists, one of which my sister works for."

That statement got a few people's attention and for a few minutes a conversation about Birthright funding was actually happening, but it quickly died amidst all the commotion. Some of the blue shirts were going around and lighting bonfires near the tents. It was never confirmed, but it sounded like some people had stolen into the desert with a boom box and were having a rave to a Lady Gaga soundtrack. Sleepily, I watched a few soldiers from our trip getting more and more cozy with the American boys and girls.

I had already witnessed many cases in which the trip design was very intentional. This night would prove to be one of the most obvious cases of the unspoken, encouraged hook-up. What else could be expected from a large-group "sleeping" arrangement in the dark desert with all our chaperones out of sight?

I could not stay awake for the social night that was beginning, and I was growing too tired to be a voyeur to the potential hook-ups in our group. I headed toward the tents and crashed hard in the corner, wrapped up tightly in a fondle-proof cocoon.

I woke up in the middle of the night to heavy breathing. I tuned it out and fell back into dreams in my dirt covered sleep-sack.

Chapter 10: Silence From Gaza to the West Bank

We loaded our bus the next morning, after having breakfast in a massive dining hall with hundreds of other kids and young adults. We were off to explore the southern part of Israel. One element of Israel Advocacy is to support the claim that Israel "made the desert bloom." After a morning hike we drove out to visit Ben Gurion's tomb, where Shai spoke highly of Israel's first prime minister.

I sat under the shade of a tree and watched a few members of our group pick up rocks and place them on the tomb, a traditional memorial among the Jewish faith. Shai spoke of David Ben Gurion's goal of integrating the Negev desert into Israel and his hopes for populating this region of Israel. Between Beer-Sheva and Eliat lies Israel's most unpopulated region, the Negev Desert. In this region, the climate is arid, hot, and was a hard sell for new settlers. It continues to be mostly unpopulated today, and the government of Israel continues to offer subsidies and initiatives to get Israelis to move to the region.

In 2008, then Prime Minister Arial Sharon implemented a ten-year plan for the region entitled "Negev 2015." This $ 3.6 billion plan would push to bring a bigger Jewish population into the desert. Currently Bedouins make up thirty percent of the desert's population, and their "unrecognized villages" are in danger of being razed. The Negev 2015 plan would demolish these villages and move the existing population to one of seven planned Bedouin "townships" in the region. Unfortunately, employment opportunities for Bedouin people were not built into the design of the townships, and those who found employment elsewhere would be forced to travel far for work.

Shai was speaking about Ben Gurion's belief that the desert could bloom life, a vision that obviously did not take the indigenous population into consideration.

After lunch in a small town with only two restaurants, we headed to our final desert destination. In order to demonstrate how life could bloom in the desert, it was arranged that we visit a farm. As we exited the bus into the dry air and sand covered earth, we walked into a fertile farm. Herbs, tomatoes, carrots, and strawberries grew in systems designed specifically for the desert climate. It was interesting to see carrots growing in the desert sands, but when I asked where the food grown on the farm went, it was made clear, this farm was just for us tourists. It wasn't providing nourishment for anyone in the region, but rather entertainment for passersby and "proof" that Israelis could make the desert bloom. I shook my head at the idea of it all as we eventually boarded the bus. This farm was built solely for the purpose of adding another destination to Birthright trips, and other trips like it, and for nourishing settler-colonialist ideology.

The farm was located six miles away from Gaza and about five miles away from Egypt. As we drove north out of the desert, we passed through some small streets with bomb shelters beside every bus stop, and finally someone addressed the elephant in the room.

"Are we near the Gaza Strip?"

Shai took a moment to answer saying only, "We are very close to Gaza. In this region of Israel, *when* rockets come over from Gaza, residents only have thirty seconds to seek shelter. That's why there are so many bomb shelters around here."

I rarely saw anyone in the streets as we drove toward the highway. It seemed to be a very desolate area.

We finally made our way to the highway and were headed north out of the desert and toward Jerusalem. We had a few hours until we arrived. I sat, dividing my attention between the window views of an endless desert landscape and casually talking with my seat buddy, Ben, when we suddenly came to a stop.

I looked out the window to see what had caused the delay. Somehow, while chatting with Ben, I had missed the change in scenery. In the once open and empty desert stood a cluster of buildings within a guarded complex with a futuristic dome shaped structure in the center. I looked at Ben only to find he had as much question in his eyes as I did. We both leaned over in the aisle to peer out of the front windshield to see why we were delayed. Shai stood up doing the same and mumbling under his breath. About one-hundred yards ahead of where we were stopped, an entourage of unmarked buses was piling out of the entrance and onto the highway. One after another, they seemed never-ending. I looked up at Shai as he reached for the microphone.

"Ok, guys. We have bad timing. It's the time of day when the shift at this textile factory gets out of work and we have to wait for everyone to leave. We'll be moving in a few minutes," he finished and put the microphone away.

Amy leaned up in her seat toward Shai.

"I don't remember seeing this when I was here before," she said. "What kind of plant is it?" she asked.

Shai looked at her and Sara and whispered, "It's a nuclear facility. This is a shift change."

Ben and I both overheard and shared a look of disbelief. We remained quiet and eavesdropped on Shai talking to the girls.

"A nuclear power plant?" one of them asked.

Shai gave them both a sarcastic look as he replied, "Yeah. Sure, and other nuclear endeavors." They both reacted with surprise as I watched the three of them share a look of parental superiority, like a parent spelling out n-a-p-t-i-m-e in the presence of their oblivious child. We were the oblivious children in this scenario.

Eventually the shift change caravan had finished and we continued north toward Jerusalem. Ben and I only shared a few more words during the commute before he nodded off and I stared deeply into the desert.

As the hours passed, the landscape changed dramatically from the flat and endless desert to winding roads in the green valleys and mountains. Our bus seemed to be climbing toward an unseen but promising destination, the last stop on our journey and where we would spend our final three nights in Israel.

As we entered the city limits, the air became less dense and the anticipation was palpable. As eager eyes wiped sleep away, Shai played the song

"Jerusalem" by the world-famous Jewish rapper Matisyahu. Everyone sat up and looked upon the new landscape as Shai spoke into the microphone.

"Welcome to Jerusalem, everybody!" he said with excitement. "This is my favorite city in Israel. It has the most life and the most spirit of any other city. Every time I come up the valley to the city I get chills."

Perhaps it was his excitement that was making the ascent into the city so exciting. Whatever it was, it was being felt by nearly everyone on the bus, including myself.

Perhaps Jerusalem did have a different energy within it than other cities we had passed through. As we moved through the center of the bustling city, I stared wide-eyed out of the window. Tons of pedestrians, orthodox-clothed kids and families ran in crosswalks to beat changing lights. Arab women in head scarves and plain-clothed people all sharing sidewalks and occasional smiles. It reminded me of New York City in its diversity. As I let the city sights saturate my thoughts, we pulled out of the street and into our hotel parking lot.

We piled out of the bus yet again and pulled our luggage from its belly toward the hotel lobby. By this point in the trip, I had befriended a couple of other girls that I found to be both tolerable and entertaining, and we chose to room together for the last three nights of our stay. Sara handed us the key, and we headed off to settle in before dinner.

In the short amount of time we had out of the group before dinner, the three of us sat talking about the "textile" factory statement Shai had made earlier. I was the only one of us who had heard him talking with Sara and Amy about it being a nuclear facility. They shook their head in disbelief and we began to share some of our gripes about the one-sidedness of the trip. Less than a half-hour after getting to the room, we were heading downstairs to meet up with everyone again.

At dinner, the serious conversation faded out to the tune of uproarious cafeteria chatter. The endless buffet of hummus and falafel continued at every destination and hotel cafeteria across Israel. As we sat eating and laughing, ignoring our sleepiness, Shai approached each table solemnly and informed us of our next scheduled meeting.

"In forty-five minutes we are going to meet in the lobby and head to a meeting room downstairs that has been set aside for us this evening." He made his announcement slowly and walked away.

I wondered why his energy had shifted so dramatically from just an hour earlier when we entered the city.

I pushed around the food on my plate, nibbling on some veggies before getting up to take my tray to be washed. A couple of friendly young Arab boys were attending the dishwasher and happily took my plate and smiled. I wandered out toward the lobby, and eventually outside, to find a group of smokers all huddled along the hotel wall near an ashtray. Most of the folks were from my group, so I found a spot among them and bummed a cigarette from Ben.

"Tomorrow we go to Yad Vashem, right?" one of the boys on our group asked.

"Yeah, so no drinking tonight!" replied our guard.

Everyone chuckled.

Our armed guard was a twenty-two year old Jerusalem native. He was excited to be in his hometown finally, but said that he could not leave us to see his family or friends until the trip was finished. Instead, he made friends with us and smoked cigarettes with the outcasts. He was a disheveled young man that many of the girls on our trip found attractive and were not afraid to let it be known. He had a growing list of lady callers that shared time with him. He did manage to maintain a distance, albeit a small one.

Yad Vashem, the Holocaust museum, was one of the biggest highlights of the Birthright trip. It was one of two days on our trip where we were not allowed to consume alcohol the night before. The other was the night before the physically exhausting climb to Masada.

We threw our cigarette butts in the ashtray and began to gather in the lobby before heading downstairs to our conference room. Sara and Amy met us there and had us count off before leading us down. The conference rooms were in the bomb shelter of the hotel basement. Each of the doorways we walked through had huge thick metal doors hanging in them. We moved through the eerie and cold space and into a room where Shai sat alone among a circle of chairs. As we entered, he quietly instructed us to take a seat. In the center of the circle of chairs, and scattered on the floor were index cards with handwritten words on them. They read, "Reality," "Loss," "Death," "Family," and so on. There were also pictures, some graphic, among the words on the floor. We filed in and became quiet very quickly. The mood called for silence. I sat almost directly opposite of Shai and watched him closely as he began to speak after some quiet moments had passed.

"Tomorrow, we will visit Yad Vashem, or the Holocaust Museum. Everyone is familiar with the Holocaust," he spoke slowly and with long pauses between statements. "For everyone here, the Holocaust evokes different emotions, or feelings," he paused again. "For others it reminds you of stories you've heard or read," he took a breath and looked around the room slowly.

I was looking at the floor, as many other were as well. I anticipated the words and images would play into some activity we would do that evening.

Shai continued, "I want to take a minute, or a few minutes if you need, and ask you to stand and move around the room. You see the images and words scattered along the floor. Just walk around them, look at them and sit back down when you find one that sticks out to you. We will take a few minutes to think about whatever it was that stood out to you, and then I'll ask you to share it with us—if you can," he finished and invited us to begin moving around the room.

Everyone stood quietly. It seemed that I wasn't the only one avoiding eye contact. Everyone seemed to be looking down or staring off into deep nothingness. All the joking around and laughter was left somewhere among the iron-clad thresholds we crossed to get into the cold room. We moved slowly and carefully. Some people knelt beside the cards and inspected them more fully, as if working to remember the pain or recall their own family stories. I found a word that stood out to me quickly and sat back down. I watched as each person took their time with the words and images. Some taking longer than others to choose their prompt. No one touched the cards. We only moved around them and knelt before them, as if they were holy. A few moments passed once we were all seated before Shai continued. The room was full of emotion and wandering eyes that never meet.

"Okay," he said, finally breaking the silence. "I'll go first and we'll move clockwise," he announced before taking a deep breath. "I chose family…"

As he spoke, I felt myself become more and more tense. I felt saddened and thoughtful as we remembered our stories or our histories, but I also felt a lot of anger. The word "Reality" stood out to me more than anything else. I sat with half open ears as I tried to find the words to say within myself to express my roaring emotions.

Another person was speaking about family as I tuned back in momentarily. Another person chose the word "reality" and spoke about how the Holocaust was a dreadful reality. I took deep breaths as I zoned out and went back to my own thoughts. I wanted to speak up for all the genocides without memorials, for the Native Americans massacred, for the Palestinians literally pushed from their homes, and for the Bedouins who worked in theme parks putting on a show for tourists. I was in a deep emotional battle with myself as the circle closed in and my turn to speak approached. Some people spoke in lingering and dreary sentences, and others kept it simple. Without a doubt, everyone seemed to be tapping into an emotional and vulnerable place.

Ben, who was often a catalyst for debate, kept his response short. He also spoke about family and how he was grateful for them despite the horrors of the Holocaust.

Suddenly, my turn was next. I was rehearsing the words in my head before I was asked to speak. I wanted to say something worthwhile since I had the floor, but something that would spark a conversation, not an argument.

I took a deep breath and began with a shaky voice.

"I chose Reality," I began slowly. "Because," I paused again out of fear but continued, "because the reality is that there are genocides occurring right now." I paused and gathered more confidence in the breath between sentences. "Because the reality is that there are millions of people dying all over this world because of injustice."

I looked out onto the faces of my trip mates and made eye contact with Ben.

"The reality is that there are tears being shed outside of this room, and I think that it would do us all more good," I paused again before finishing. "I think it would do us all more good if we didn't abide by the slogan 'Never Forget' and instead we lived by the slogan 'Get Involved.'"

I paused only briefly before saying, "I hope that the memories we are sharing here open everyone up to other injustices and that you feel inspired to explore human rights issues beyond only remembering Jewish people who were killed during the Holocaust."

I finished, half expecting an uproar, but was met only with silence. The sharing circle continued without any hesitation. I took deep breath of relief and met eyes with Brian for a moment. He raised his eyebrows in some sort of small congratulations and I nodded slightly in appreciation.

It was becoming clear that there were some more educated persons in our group who were eager to talk about Palestine, among other political issues. We would soon open up to each other about how we could not believe there was never even a mention of Palestine. Even if I didn't say exactly what I wanted to with the words I spoke, I could tell that I said enough to speak to those few who were longing for a real and open conversation about this ever-present conflict.

As the circle closed, Shai took the floor again, giving us instructions for the next morning. No one spoke as we headed out of the bomb shelter and toward our rooms, leaving Shai alone to pick up his index cards off the cold tile floor.

As we approached the elevators, my roommates and I found each other and squeezed in. We got off on the third floor and broke away from the group.

"I can't believe we haven't talked about Palestine yet," Angelica whispered to us as we walked in and closed the door to our room.

Chapter 11: Yad Vashem and Holocaust Guilt

The bus was mostly quiet as we moved through the early morning streets of Jerusalem toward Yad Vashem, Israel's Holocaust Museum. Brian had casually taken the seat beside me as we boarded the bus a few minutes earlier. Amongst the hum of the engine and the low chatter of a few conversations, Brian and I eased into a discussion of our expectations of the day. We spoke about the previous night's activity and the emotionally palatable scene we had witnessed.

"I liked what you said last night," Brian began.

I knew there was connection of shared beliefs when we exchanged glances the night before, though this confirmed it.

"I felt as if there was no better word to pick, and I hope that in what little I said, at least someone understands what I was really trying to say," I explained. "The Holocaust was horrendous," I said quietly, "but I don't agree with the use of it as a means of invoking nationalism, especially under these circumstances." I finished quieter.

Brian silently nodded, appearing to understand my brief and vague statements. I felt a rush of anxiety and relief. We spoke excitedly of our opinions of the trip so far, and agreed there was strong emotional manipulation in the activity that Shai had led last night.

As we pulled into the driveway of the museum, Brian leaned in and nearly whispered, "Have you heard of Finklestein?"

I shot up in excitement. "Yes!" I proclaimed with restraint.

Before my journey to Israel, I watched an interesting and moving video of professor and author Norman Finkelstein yelling at a young American

Jewish student who began crying while trying to explain her sympathies with Israel because of the crimes of the Holocaust. In the video, Finkelstein shuts down this young woman's argument by refusing to accept her "crocodile tears" and the atrocities of Holocaust as justification for the "torture [...] and brutalization by Israel against the Palestinians." It was a thought-provoking video that stuck with me throughout the trip. I would later read Finkelstein's book, *The Holocaust Industry*, in which he speaks further on this idea. "The Holocaust...proved to be a perfect weapon for deflecting criticism of Israel." And further, "The Holocaust proved to be a potent ideological weapon."[1] I suspected that Shai's energy shift had something to do with our journey to Yad Vashem the next day.

We spoke of the video and agreed firmly against the use of one atrocity to justify another. I shared with him my observations of the crying girls during our trip to the Tel-Aviv museum.

"It scares me to see the need to cry in some people," I revealed. "I expect by the end of today, many tears will be shed, and in part because of emotional manipulation," I finished solemnly.

I had uncovered a sleepy excitement in my brain as we connected in our shrewd criticism. My excitement was soon hushed as Shai began to speak.

"Okay everyone, today is going to be a very emotional day," he began bluntly. "I will escort you to the door, and if I feel up for it, I may join you, but it is often too emotional for me." He paused as we came to a stop in the parking lot. "You will have a Yad Vashem tour guide today who will take you through the museum. It is very big, but he will take you through most of it on a journey through many parts of the Holocaust," he finished and we began unloading without transition.

Our group filed in toward the entrance. I let many people slip by me as I walked slowly beside Brian. We had taken up the rear of the group and maintained an almost observational distance from everyone else. As we were being handed headsets from our new tour guide, I noticed that Shai had not made it in with us. We pulled the devices over our ears and clipped the receiver to our pants.

"Is everyone here?" a voice cracked in through the headphones.

1 Norman Finkelstein, *The Holocaust Industry: Reflections on the Exploitation of Jewish Suffering*. (London: Verso, 2003), 31.

I looked up to see our tour guide's lips moving along to the words in my ears and nodded a confirmation in his direction.

We began by standing over a model replica of the building we were in. I watched the faces of my companions carefully. Our guide explained the museum's design to us.

"The thin and linear design is to assure that guests would move forward through the exhibits and not get lost or move backwards. There is a chronological progression of the story in Yad Vashem. It would take an entire day to really absorb and see all the parts and exhibits of the museum, but we only have a few hours."

With that, we began to follow him through the Yad Vashem experience. Brian and I maintained our distance without speaking. We moved along through the sleek and tall granite halls as a bulbous mass, attempting to avoid collisions with other groups like ours. Our guide paused in exhibits and addressed us with an ever-changing energy. At times, he spoke with stillness, while at others, he was emotionally charged and dynamic. His voice carried along in our ears even if we were out sight. I moved slowly around each exhibit while he spoke as an actor toward an audience. After a few minutes in each exhibit, he would beckon us on to another artifact or room.

The soldiers, who were still with us on this part of our trip, were required to dress in uniform during the day's activities. Each one was visibly bored. On occasion, I would make eye contact with a soldier and the bored look would transform to the fake attentiveness of a grade school student caught doodling.

Over an hour had passed as we made our way through the museum and through the history of the Holocaust. I took a seat in a silent viewing room away from our group, but was still able to hear the tour guide speak in my headset. He was explaining the conditions for Jews in ghettos during World War II. I leaned back against the wall in the empty viewing room and got lost within my thoughts. The black and white projection danced across the screen as I wondered about other non-Jewish victims of this genocide. What about the nearly half a million Roma that were massacred by hands of Nazis during the Holocaust? We were shown no exhibits of the handicapped, who were the first to be murdered by the Nazi regime, or of the homosexuals and dark-skinned Roma who were rounded up into ghettos alongside the Jews. We were being told to "Never Forget," but only a Jewish suffering was to receive our remembrance here. I felt a deep sadness fill me as I was jerked out of my thoughts and back into reality. Brian had found me to tell me our group had moved along. He sensed my uneasiness and respected it by walking beside me in silence. Nearly everyone in our group was silent. A sight unseen since before we left the U.S.

We caught up with our guide as he entered into the "Righteous Among the Nations" exhibit. This hall is dedicated to gentiles (non-Jewish persons) who helped Jews escape during the Holocaust. Our guide told the tale of one of the "righteous" as I looked through some of the artifacts in the exhibit. This room would be the one and only mention of non-Jewish persons during our visit that day.

"Acting beyond fear, the righteous took in persecuted Jewish people and offered them shelter, resources, safety, and, at times, would help them with obtaining papers or escape. For these acts of sheer bravery, Yad Vashem and the state of Israel honors them as the 'righteous among the nations,'" our guide said while wrapping up his speech for this room.

As we moved out of one space into another, I lingered to read a placard on the wall:

"The Yad Vashem Law authorizes Yad Vashem to confer honorary citizenship of the State of Israel upon the Righteous Among the Nations and commemorative citizenship if they have passed away."

I walked away without looking at anything else and followed slowly behind the rest of our group. I shook my head at the thought that the state would grant a deceased non-Jewish person "commemorative citizenship" and yet deny so many living, indigenous, Palestinian inhabitants of the land any such recognition while simultaneously working everyday to impose every conceivable limit upon their lives and livelihood.

I noticed that Brian was standing next to me as we entered a brilliant, light-filled room. The entire museum up to this point was dark and gray, cold and uninviting, and evoked feelings of physical discomfort and, at times, mild claustrophobia. However, this room was gigantic, open, golden, and flooded with light. In the center of the open space was a pit of light with a glass barricade around its rim. We gathered around the glass wall and leaned on it peering up. Above our heads and the hole in the floor was a huge dome filled with pictures, words, and white light. Hundreds of images of Jews lost during the Holocaust were arranged among the light cone above us.

Surrounding us were half-empty metal shelves of binders. I felt the shift in mood almost immediately. It was a profound and moving presentation. I felt an emotional response to the room, to the change in the use of light, to the vastness of the seemingly never-ending cone of light and death above us. As I recognized these emotions rising in me, I released my cold grip from the glass wall and stepped a few steps back and out of the experience.

Our tour guide began talking, vibrantly yet solemnly. He introduced the "Hall of Names," pointed out the massive floor-to-ceiling shelves filled with binders of murdered Jews' names and histories. Many rows of shelves were unoccupied, which he explained were for those lost, which will never be found, whose stories would never be remembered. He continued talking about the research team that works to tell the stories of those killed during the Holocaust and encouraged us to use the databases around to look up our families.

I stood now, many feet behind my group and our guide, I had lost sight of Brian as I became a voyeur to my companions. I watched the silence. I watched their staring eyes dart from picture to picture above their craned necks. I saw two girls fall into each other as if on cue and drench one another in tears. I watched tears well up in the least vulnerable and the least expected of my group. Those unable to cry stood with bowed heads, in the way you grieve the death of someone you did not know. Tear soaked hands left streaks and fingerprints on the glass wall they leaned on. I turned my head from the group and looked stoically toward the empty shelves. I too felt a shame, but not the childlike shame one might feel when unaffected by a tragedy everyone perceives as deeply tangible.

When I was a teenager in rural Georgia, I was invited to a haunted house organized by a local church. It was unlike any haunted house I had been to before or since. In each room was a different life tragedy: a drunk driver after a crash, a teen on the verge of suicide, an overdosing anorexic. The rooms were replete with actors whose sole job was to fill viewers with a deep and unrelenting fear. At the end of the haunted house, we filed into a bright room and were joined by the pastor of the church. He spoke warmly as light danced around his figure. He invited anyone who wished to be saved up to the altar to receive Jesus Christ as their savior. Laden with fear and shame, many teens pulled their way toward the front and took part in the ritual. I stood removed then much as I had in the "Hall of Names," filled with the same feeling of shame.

Although the atrocities of the Holocaust quite understandably evoke strong feelings of collective grief, I stood ashamed knowing that human vulnerability can be used to shape the political and religious ideology through the use of fear, shame, and spectacle.

The teary-eyed regained their composure as we walked out of the museum and into the courtyard. The sun offered a refreshing natural warmth after being inside for the past few hours. I put on my sunglasses and wandered around the courtyard as we all waited to be reunited with Shai. I walked over to a wall and leaned into it as I thought about the "experience" of Yad Vashem so far. I watched my group mates mingle, some still emotional, others already shedding the heaviness of the whole morning. Beyond my companions on the opposing wall of the courtyard, I noticed around a dozen guns leaned against the wall. The sight of this caught my attention and pulled me out of my own thoughts. I peered through our group to see a dozen or more young faces in fatigues slouched along the wall and eating from brown sack lunch bags, nearly the same color as their uniforms. Their guns, M16 assault rifles, leaned against the wall next to the snacking teens as they spoke fervently in Hebrew. It was an ordinary lunch break for the young IDF soldiers. I looked toward Brian and Ben who were talking near me and nodded in the directions of the guns and soldiers. They shared my surprise at the casualness of stacked guns next to a group of chatty teens.

"When I was eighteen," I began but didn't need to finish.

We shook our heads at our culture shock and the evidence of such a highly militarized society.

Shai was back with us, and, before we had time to react fully, we were being escorted into another building of Yad Vashem to hear a Holocaust survivor's story.

I took a seat in the back of the classroom and leaned on the desktop. I was sleepy and the room was warm. Sun streamed in from the window beside me and it felt like a blanket wrapped around my shoulders. I was not alone in my revelry of sitting in a warm room. Many faces looked tired, and, after walking through the museum for so long, it was a nice reprieve to sit.

The Holocaust survivor who would address us was actually the grandmother of one of the people in our group, who was born in Israel but raised in the United States and had been to Israel many times to visit his grandmother and family. Birthright is open to any Jew between eighteen and twenty-six years old who has not lived in Israel past the age of twelve. Though he had been back many times, he still qualified for Birthright.

It was a surprise to all of us that his grandmother would be sharing her story, and suddenly the fatigue was forced to take a back seat, yet again. He introduced her to us and hugged her sweetly before she began her story.

She was a young girl during her story, between five and nine years old. She told it with great details and imagery. She described the snow's depth, the thinness of the winter air, her emotional state, and many other details that one often forgets when so young. She spoke slowly over the course of an hour or more. It was a powerful story.

In the end of her story, she did not go back to her birthplace and she did not flee to the United States or another country; she made her home Israel. Her surviving family, fleeing persecution during the Holocaust, found refuge in Israel, a country that was theoretically designed to offer the persecuted a home and safety. Her story would have evoked a sense of national pride among our group no matter which country it was. Yet, she could only offer us Israeli pride, and it was well received.

She finished and hugged her grandson during the applause. Many people went to meet her and to thank her for her story before leaving the classroom.

I walked out into the hallway with a few others who went rushing toward the bathrooms after sitting silent and unstirring for over an hour, out of respect of our trip mate's grandmother. There are many Holocaust survivor stories, each with different endings and details.

Hajo Meyer, who was one of the last remaining survivors of Auschwitz until his death in late 2014, found his home in the Netherlands after the Holocaust. He spent a great deal of his later years working on anti-Zionist projects, including writing a book titled *The End of Judaism,* as well as touring the world with his message of support for Palestinian freedom. In his book, Meyer argues that Israel uses the atrocities of the Holocaust to justify Zionism, Israel, and the same types of indecent crimes against Palestinians. In an interview with Electronic Intifada shortly before his death, Meyer held fast that Israel's treatment of Palestinians was inhumane, saying, "If we want to stay really human beings, we must get up and call the Zionists what they are: Nazi criminals."[2]

Meyer, unlike our presenter, drew upon his Holocaust experience to call out Israel on abusing Holocaust guilt on the world Jewry in favor of Zionism. Unfortunately, this sort of message would not be heard on our trip.

I was staring deeply into a snack machine as the rest of my trip mates filed out of the classroom. There were more hugs and thanks as we exited the building and entered back into the warming Jerusalem afternoon. Shai started a count off as we stood outside.

"One."

"Two."

"Three."

And so on.

After we had finished counting and all parties were accounted for, one of the quieter girls on our trip made a timid remark.

"Does anyone else think it's a little inappropriate to be counting off Jews outside of Yad Vashem?"

A few folks chuckled uncomfortably, but during Birthright, we were more often numbers than we were names.

After lunch, and yet another nameless count-off, the forty-five of us loaded up the bus and headed to Mount Herzl, Israel's national cemetery.

The day's obligatory sadness continued as we spent the gloomy yet sun-filled afternoon wandering through gravesites of Israel's national heroes. In general, the mood of my travel companions was gleeful and light-hearted, however, that mood was stashed somewhere else today. Words were rarely spoken as we walked through Mount Herzl's monuments, stopping every so often to hear Shai speak about whatever site we were overlooking.

My attention waned through most of the visit, until we found ourselves at the gravesite of American IDF soldier Michael Levin.

Shai began to tell us about the lone soldier, a term used for any non-Israeli Jew who comes alone to Israel to join their army. Levin made Aliyah to Israel in 2002 at only eighteen years old. In 2006, his unit was sent into

2 Adri Nieuwhof, "In last interview, Auschwitz survivor urged Palestinians 'not to give up their fight.'" *Electronic Intifada*. 25 August 2014. https://electronicintifada.net/blogs/adri-nieuwhof/last-interview-auschwitz-survivor-urged-palestinians-not-give-their-fight

battle in Lebanon during the month-long conflict between Israel and Lebanon. Over one thousand casualties were recorded during the conflict that was eventually ended by United Nations intervention. Among the deceased was Michael Levin.

Shai told us that he was originally not allowed to join his unit because he was a lone soldier, yet after fighting for his right to serve Israel, he was given the go-ahead to join them. He died in that battle in 2006. His gravesite is now, according to Shai, visited by thousands of people annually. There were countless tokens, rocks, and notes on his grave. I stood behind his gravestone examining some of the tokens left behind as Shai continued to talk about Levin's service to Israel. I looked up at the Israeli soldiers who continued to look as bored as they did while in Yad Vashem. I looked over to the female soldier that had once worn the "Been There, Done That" t-shirt. Since that day, we would routinely lock eyes during one of our many tourist visits and she would have the same smirk on her face. However, on this day, she only gazed boringly at the grass, a look that most of her fellow soldiers shared with her as Shai went on about lone soldiers.

In July of 2014, another young American lone soldier died while serving in the IDF.

Max Weinberg, who went on Birthright in 2012, had also visited Levin's grave. Upon his death, his family recalled that he had no original interest to go on the Birthright tour, however, he gave in after his siblings convinced him to join them. Pictures of his visit to Levin's grave surfaced in the media after his death and his family agreed that upon returning from Birthright he was convinced he must serve in the Israeli army. There was no conclusive evidence to suggest it was the visit to Mount Hertzl or Levin's grave that persuaded Weinberg to move to Israel, but the Birthright trip cost him his life.

It is no secret that Birthright organizers share excitement around those who make Aliyah. Taglit, the parent organization of Birthright, has funded numerous independent studies in the past five years that measure impact in order to legitimize their organization. Around the time of Weinberg's death in 2014, Birthright estimated that twenty to thirty thousand of its alumni had moved to Israel. Max Weinberg was one of them until his untimely death in Gaza.

Making Aliyah can be a complex but rewarding proposal for American Jews. Comfortable "absorption packets" provided by the state often assist in convincing those on the fence about making the commitment to Israel. Aliyah was often talked about during Birthright. Sara and Amy encouraged us daily to talk to them about programs that could bring us back to Israel.

We continued through the graveyard through most of the afternoon. Faces got longer as posture got poorer. Everyone was visibly bored or tired from our long day. We finally boarded the bus and headed to a nearby shook, or open-air market, before we headed back to the hotel. We were given less than an hour of free time before we were rounded up for dinner and our evening mifgash activity. I strolled away from the group and disappeared among the pedestrians on a cobblestone street in Jerusalem.

As I wandered alone I noticed the variety of people who lived in this ancient city. Muslims in traditional wear did their shopping beside Orthodox Jews. For a moment, I was reminded again of New York City. Yet amidst such diversity, we only spoke of one side, of one people. On my lonesome stroll as I witnessed people hurry along their daily lives, I was hopeful for that night's mifgash activity.

Shai announced on the bus before we got to the shook that the soldiers would be facilitating an activity for us that evening. They had hoped to talk about what it's like to be a young Israeli and have an open discussion. He promised they had worked hard on their plan for the evening and that it would be rewarding. After yet another day of lectures, I looked forward to having an open dialog with my peers. This was their final night with us on our trip. I was hopeful this would mean they would come to our final activity with unabashed honesty and talk freely, for once, about politics in Israel.

I rounded the corner and headed back toward the bus after purchasing some dates and spices from a local merchant. As I walked up the cobblestone path that had led me to more optimistic thoughts, I noticed a rush of my trip mates at a liquor kiosk. A group of ten or more was shoved inside the tiny liquor store. They were quickly making final purchases before our rendezvous time, which, coincidentally, was right at that very moment. I walked hurriedly past them and toward the other punctual group members that had already reconvened. Shai peered down the cobblestone path as we waited for the rest of the group to arrive.

An hour had proven to be enough time for shopping and the plastic-bagged evidence rattled around the lively bus. It was the first time that day that I had seen everyone without languorous looks. Bags of olives, pastries, wines, and liquors had revived the spirit of our group as we headed toward dinner and our final evening with the soldiers.

Brian sat with me and we chatted about nothing in particular as we showed each other the rugelach and red wine we planned on consuming later that evening. I asked what he thought the soldiers had planned for our evening.

"Oh," he said remembering the promise Shai had made earlier. "I don't know, but maybe we can finally talk about something real?" he finished with hopeful pondering.

"Maybe Palestine? Maybe anything political?" I predicted.

Angelica and Ben were in the seat behind us and both leaned forward to join our conversation.

"Yes, that would be awesome," Angelica delivered between the crack in the seat.

Ben peeked over the top of our chairs.

"I think they're gonna talk about Palestine issues, finally." Ben said. "I heard them talking with Shai at lunch," he finished.

We each rose our eyebrows in surprise and sunk back into our seats.

Finally. No more after-dinner lectures. No more guilt-induced soul searching. Finally, we were going to have a real conversation about Palestine.

We had about an hour after dinner to ourselves before the conversation. My roommates and I sat around eating some of the snacks we had procured that afternoon when there was a knock on the door. Ben and Brian were standing there with a deck of cards and a bottle of wine. We quickly ushered them in. We all sat around drinking, eating more, and ignoring the card game we had originally gathered to play.

"I wonder what the soldiers even have to say about Palestine," Angelica thought aloud.

She had spent a good amount of time in other parts of the Middle East before this trip and told us how she was advised to not mention her trip to Lebanon while she was in Israel.

"So, I call it Disneyland while I'm here," she joked. "And, when I was at Disneyland, they talked about Palestine and Middle Eastern politics all the time," she said holding back her laughter.

"Did the Disneyland map have accurate Palestinian borders?" I asked sarcastically.

We all burst into laughter, which was quickly thwarted as we realized how much time had passed. We had been so caught up in our conversation that we failed to realize we were almost five minutes late for the meeting. We quickly drank what wine was left in our flimsy plastic hotel cups and rushed downstairs to the fallout shelter.

We were stifling laughter as we rushed down the cinder block corridor from the elevator. We had almost walked into the wrong room where an obviously somber discussion was happening. I imagined it was similar to the emotional journey that we had experienced the night before. We came upon the open door as our group mates were pulling chairs into a circle. We sat down in what spots were available in the circle, scattered out among our colleagues.

The mood in the room was bright and full of laughter, the complete opposite of the day's heavy tone. I noticed the soldiers dressed more casually than I had seen them before. They seemed more like co-members of our generation. As we settled into our seats and quieted down, I felt an unspoken cease-fire between our soldier companions and myself.

Shai stood smiling at the ease of the evening.

"Okay guys," he began with his usual greeting. "I know today has been long and full of a lot of emotions for some of you. I was talking with the soldiers before you all came downstairs about the conversation that was planned for tonight and we agreed," he paused to clear his throat. "We agreed that it was such a heavy day that we didn't want to have a heavy conversation tonight."

He paused as he looked for a way to pass it over to the soldiers for further explanation.

"So, instead of a conversation they've decided to show you what life in Israel is like through some games. Anyways, I'll let them tell you more."

He finished and quickly sulked back into his chair and pushed himself back, slightly out of the circle.

I sat in aggravation and confusion. What the hell were games going to truly tell us about Israel, or more importantly, Palestine? I reconsidered the cease-fire.

I looked over to Brian and Ben, who up until this point had shared the same optimism about tonight as I had. We exchanged short looks of grief but were interrupted by one of the female soldiers who finally took the center of the circle to explain.

"Okay, like Shai said," she began in her Israeli accent, "we are going to play some games. These are typical Israeli games that we want to share with you and we think they will help you understand us better."

She finished with a twisted laugh.

Whatever they had planned was sure to reveal very little about being Israeli. That truth was evident in her corrupt laughter. Little did I know, I was only experiencing the beginning of what would soon become growing and obvious discontent and disgust with what games they had chosen to play.

We began with a silly children's game called Mummy, likely found in many countries, in which you wrap someone from head-to-toe in toilet paper. The first team to wrap their mummy completely wins. It was a harmless game that was a minimal-effort attempt at team building and likely did more damage to the environment than to my morale. Also, my team won.

While I have as much fun in childlike escapist activities as any weary-eyed adult, I was still uncertain how the night's games might unfold into anything meaningful.

For our next game, we were asked to sit among the strands of loose toilet paper littering the floor. The soldiers plotted giddily in a corner of the room before turning around. In one's hands were a bunch of straws. My first thought was, "Kiss and Blow" and my palm went directly to my face. I held my head in my hand and emoted a sound of audible frustration.

"We're going to play Pass the Straw!" they announced excitedly.

I had no idea what that was, but imagined it still involved mouths and potential kissing situations.

"In this game you take the straw in your mouth and pass it onto someone else. Once they have it in their mouth, you have to cut off the piece remaining in your mouth. The shorter it gets…" the announcer of the teenage erotica game paused. "The harder it gets," he finished with a smirk.

I was correct.

I shivered. I was feeling grossed out and annoyed. I immediately declined participation. Not solely on the grounds of being too mature for bullshit hook-up games, but also out of sheer disappointment for the unraveling of my expectations. I sat sulking with my arms folded as I was approached with a straw.

"Ummm, no thanks," I rapped and was quickly left alone.

I had guessed by this point in the trip the soldiers had already clumped me in with a few others as most likely to not put out. I was happy to win this superlative and remained pushed back in my chair and looked on with judgment.

I noticed Shai looked equally displaced and un-entertained by the antics unfolding.

They wrapped up the straw game and laughed over a few "close calls."

As the soldiers gathered themselves for another game, I felt a brooding presence in the seat beside me. A young man, also on the trip from New York, had taken the seat and seemed as annoyed as me.

"What the fuck?" I said looking over and expressing my aggravation.

"Yeah," he sighed. "I have a girlfriend at home. I don't want any part of kissing games," he explained.

I noticed that Ben had taken the seat on the other side of me. He did not have a girlfriend, but I still looked over and said, "What the fuck?"

He smiled and pushed his glasses up.

"I know. It's fun, but what the hell happened to 'serious conversation,'" the guy next to me uttered.

"I think this is the type of 'serious conversation' they wanted to start," I answered.

"Excuse me. Are you single and ready to mingle?" I said mockingly.

We laughed as they explained the next game.

"Okay guys! In this next game we place two seats back to back. We will take one guy and one girl volunteer."

"Heteronormative," I coughed toward Ben.

He chuckled under his breath.

"We will count to three and you will have to look either to your right or your left. If you look the opposite way, the girl will get to slap the guys face!" she explained.

The girls in the room made a collective *ooohhhh* sound.

"But!" she continued, "If you look the same way, then girls you have to kiss the guy!" She finished.

The interested boys in our group began to whoop and holler in premature victory.

I continued to hold my face in extreme discontent. I could not hide it anymore. I believe I was even shaking my head. This time I did not have to decline participation. It was understood that I was not into it. They tried to pull the faithful gentleman beside me into the game and he had to verbally decline several times before he was left alone.

While I must admit that I enjoyed seeing a fair number of gentleman get slapped, it was not worth the awkwardness of the whole experience.

The evening wrapped up with Shai making some announcement that went unnoticed due to the heightened sexual arousal of more than half of our group. We were dismissed. The soldiers mingled among the eager and made plans to meet in certain rooms when certain coasts were clear. I found myself walking with the same few I had come down there with. Our evening had unfolded much differently than anticipated. We all agreed to go back up, open another bottle of wine, eat rugelach, and actually get to the card game we had planned on earlier. After all, it was becoming obvious that we would never have an open and honest discussion about Palestine on this trip.

Chapter 12: The Western Wall and the End of Mifgash

It was nearing the end of our trip and most folks had already shed the tears they had expected. The itinerary for the final two days was quieter and slower paced than our previous non-stop days. It was a Friday morning, meaning we would have to finish up our activities by sunset in preparation for Shabbat. It was also the final day with the soldiers, from whom we had learned so little. I anticipated we would never see them again. We ventured into the Jerusalem morning after breakfast and headed toward the City of David.

We unloaded the bus and were immediately soaked with the full morning sun. Ben was particularly excited to walk around the Old City, a part of Jerusalem divided into four distinct quarters, the Jewish, Armenian, Christian, and Muslim Quarter. Though I assumed we would only get to walk around the Jewish Quarter, I was excited too. I had watched a short documentary on this part of Jerusalem before I left New York and was eager to see it with my own eyes.

Shai was far ahead of us and moving expertly through the sandstone colored architecture. He led his snake-chain tour group up the streets and ascended a set of stairs that let us out onto a beautiful lookout point. We gathered around the space admiring the hilly city of Jerusalem. I leaned both elbows on the wall and stared out into the distance. Shai, who was usually ready to spout off a list of facts about our surroundings, was busy talking with Amy and Sara. They huddled in intense conversation for some minutes as we looked around the landscape. After a few minutes Shai turned toward us and pointed at a few landmarks as he flipped through some papers. We were overlooking the Dome of the Rock, an elaborate Islamic temple with strict limitations on non-Muslim visitors and, for reasons involving Jewish Law and politics, a place where Jews are often not permitted entry.

Shai remained preoccupied for a few minutes as we chatted among ourselves. Eventually, he stopped shuffling papers and stopped to look out over the city with us. He stood quietly beside Ben and myself.

"What's that part of Jerusalem?" Ben asked Shai, pointing past the golden plated dome.

"That's Silwan, it's a Palestinian neighborhood," he answered curtly and walked over to Sara and Amy.

"Whoa, he said Palestine," I said to Ben, half joking.

It may have only been the second time he mentioned Palestine on our trip.

"I saw a movie before I came here," I explained to Ben. "It was about these Palestinian neighborhoods in Jerusalem that are being occupied by Jewish settlers, and that's probably one of them," I said nodding toward the neighborhood.

"What's that?" one of our trip mates, who had overheard us talking, asked curiously.

"It's a Palestinian neighborhood," I said pointing over. "I bet the state of Israel would pay you to move there if you make Aliyah," I said as I walked away.

Silwan, as it turns out, is in fact one of the neighborhoods in which Jewish settlers are moving into with some assistance from the state of Israel. For years, Jewish settlers have been purchasing land and homes from evicted Palestinians and settling in neighborhoods like Silwan. The evictions, land grabs, and settlements are often made possible through loopholes in the law and have faced international scrutiny. As a part of this practice, Jewish settlers often move stealthily into these homes in the middle of the night. When dawn comes, Palestinians find their new neighbors' home draped in Israeli flags and fortified with cameras and armed guards. These armed guards and surveillance cameras are compliments of the State of Israel, who in 2013 had a $19.2 million budget for settler security in East Jerusalem.

In late 2014, Silwan made the news again after approximately two hundred Jewish settlers moved into twenty-five apartments in the middle of the night. A few weeks later, dozens more settlers moved into two homes in central Silwan, again, in the middle of the night.

Before we could rouse up a conversation on the topic, we were being funneled back down the staircase and into the streets. We walked a few blocks, mostly in silence, before we came across the entrance to the City of David. We walked through the archways and into the site. It was already crawling with tourists and guided groups. Shai maintained a look of hurried aggravation as he maneuvered around the hordes and headed toward the ticket booth. We spread out seeking shade as we waited for further instruction. This tourist destination was like nearly every other place we had been before. There was a gift shop near the entrance that a few group members went into to cool down. They emerged minutes later with ice cream, and rejoined us as Shai made his way back over.

"Okay guys," he said addressing us. "Look, it's really crowded here so we have to move fast to get to everything on our agenda for the day," he said with a tinge of annoyance.

As usual, it was uncomfortably hot in the sun, it was crowded, and there were lines for every attraction.

Shai moved us through hordes of people as quickly as he could. He was mostly quiet as he hurried us along. We descended a shady staircase covered in pink flowers and turned the corner to find another line in front of our destination.

"Okay guys, just wait here," he instructed as he walked through the crowd to the next ticket counter.

We were at the entrance for the underground water tunnels, a labyrinth of knee-high flowing water that runs under the City of David. Shai demonstrated his tour guide seniority and negotiated a quicker entrance for our group. We passed by two other groups who had been waiting before we ever came downstairs and entered into the slick stone tunnels.

Shai moved us as swiftly as he could through the slippery tunnels, but it was dark, wet, and dangerous to move too quickly. He stopped at the mouth of our first descent to tell us about history of the City of David before we continued on. The quick tour took much longer than anticipated, and the knee-high water turned out to be waist high for some. After nearly two hours of zigzagging through the dark and claustrophobic tunnels, we emerged back into daylight. There was more than enough complaining and wetness for one day, and my shoes and pants were soaked up to my hips. We moved our drenched bodies toward the sunny spots in an attempt to dry off as we walked back toward the exit.

"At least now we can walk around for a bit and dry out in the Old City," Ben said excitedly.

Shai had us stand near the exit for a few minutes while he quietly talked again with Amy and Sara. After a few minutes the three of them approached the group again.

"Okay guys, the tunnel took a lot longer than I thought it would and we still have to go to the Western Wall today so we are going to have to skip the Old City," he announced.

Ben let out a deep moan of dissatisfaction.

"I know some of you really wanted to see the Old City, but we are running out of daylight. I'll point out a few things as we walk to the Western Wall," he offered in consolation.

Ben was visibly upset and there were gripes about choosing the tunnels over the Old City, but, like the entire trip, Shai called the shots and often did not inform us until the last second about our actual itinerary.

A few minutes later we began on our way toward the Western Wall. Ben walked close to Shai to ask him about landmarks we passed, and I kept a short distance behind the two. After less than thirty minutes, I was nearly dry in the heat of the waxing afternoon.

The Western Wall, or Wailing Wall, was the last destination on our trip that would pull any tears from the eyes of our group. It is considered one of the holiest places among the Jewish faithful, and thousands of tourists make the pilgrimage annually. It is a site often visited by Jews at least once in their lifetime. Though I did not feel spiritually tied to the stone structure, it was a significant historical landmark that peeked my interest. My grandparents, whom I barely knew, had been to this place, and that connection meant a lot to me. My grandmother unexpectedly died in her fifties after her diabetes medication attacked her kidneys. I was young when she passed and only got to know her posthumously through stories my mother told us. She was a brash English teacher who married a man with five kids and raised them in the desert wasteland of Las Vegas. She lived on in stories, photos, and symbols. As we approached the wall, I thought mostly of her.

Shai led us toward an entrance with a sign that read, "Tour Groups Must Use Other Entrance." He ushered us forward, ignoring the sign. There were separate entrances for men and women. The guys in our group went to the left and the girls to the right. It was approaching late afternoon as we filed in the entrances. Shai was talking wildly in Hebrew to a worker at the gate that was clearly opposed to our use of this entrance, yet we continued on. We huddled near the gates and waited for everyone to make their way inside.

"Okay guys, as you noticed when we entered, the wall is separated by gender. Men may visit the wall on the left and women on the right," he informed us. "It is customary after praying at the wall to walk backwards and to not turn your back to the wall as you walk away. Sometimes there are 'moral police,' usually older hassidic jews who will give you a hard time if you don't walk backwards," Shai explained to us using air quotes. "Also, you will see in the cracks hundreds of pieces of paper. These are filled with prayers. You should feel free to add your prayer to the wall if you find a space."

He paused for a moment before he dismissed us.

"This is a holy place," he said and paused pensively. "Millions of people have touched this wall before you, so even if you don't pray in your everyday life, this is still a holy place. Thousands of hands have brushed along the stones you will touch, so many hands that in places the stone is smooth."

He paused again.

"Even if you don't pray, I think you should at least touch the wall," he finished, and with that we were silently dismissed.

It was wretchedly hot and there was no shade to be found. I walked slowly and alone toward the entrance labeled "Women." I let everyone in our group move ahead of me. I lingered far from the wall on our segregated side and watched women stream past me and fall into prayer. I stood out of the way and in the sun for some time as I grappled with the implications of going forward to touch this holy site.

I was both intrigued and disenchanted by its significance. I wanted to touch it for the mere fact of touching something so sought out and in memory of grandmother. I stood and watched fully covered Haredi woman next to tourists in shorts and t-shirts approach the wall, pray, and slowly walk backwards away from it. At first I only spotted one woman walking backwards, then I noticed another, and another fall in step with her.

I lifted my eyes toward a wooden walkway overhead.

In the wooden boxed walkway, which began at ground level and ramped up nearly one hundred yards to the top of the wall, stood an innumerable amount of black-masked Israeli soldiers. They stood from its barricaded entrance at the ground all the way to the top of wall. Some were standing languorously and even leaning on the wooden slats with their machine guns dangling at their sides. They peered out among the visitors through the eyeholes in their black bank-robber masks. I stood now fixated on this sight. Why were there dozens of black masked, heavily armed, Israeli soldiers standing above us in a wooden planked box? I caught eyes with one of the soldiers and quickly looked away in fear. I looked around to see if anyone else had caught sight of the soldiers as they lurked overhead. I found no one who seemed to find it an odd sight. I looked among masses to find even more women shuffling backwards, including some from my group.

I sighed, turned away, and walked even further from the wall. Experiencing the Wailing Wall was not enough to outweigh the reality of a backward-pacing military state. I took a seat near the entrance and waited for our group to finish their prayers and reassemble.

Eventually, we were all standing together and began counting off. We were forty-five for the last time on that count. The soldiers were leaving us and ending the mifgash portion of our trip.

"Okay guys, listen," Shai said. "This is where the soldiers leave us, so why don't we let them say their goodbyes away from the crowd before we move on," he said as he moved us all toward a sun drenched space near the exit.

We gathered in a circle and let the soldiers speak about their experience during mifgash with our group. I had formed no particular bonds with any one of them and was unemotional during their departure. They exited with us and then went on their way, leaving behind a few shameful memories of high-school-style hook-up attempts.

We counted off again, this time only thirty-nine. As we went around shouting numbers toward the sky, I noticed even more guards on the ground. About forty soldiers were standing within a metal barricade in heavy armor with their guns at attention. They had not been there when we arrived. The count had finished and we began moving toward the exit. I walked quickly toward the front to be near Shai.

"Hey, what's with all the guards back there?" I asked before we made it to the exit. He turned to look at where I was pointing.

"It's a Muslim holiday today, so there's more security," he answered simply.

I shook my head as I fell back out of step with him. He did little to explain the excessive police presence. I later found out from our guard that during Muslim holidays, Israel refuses West Bank Palestinians entry into Jerusalem.

We filed into the street and were greeted almost immediately by our bus. We climbed in and made our way out of the Old City and back toward our hotel.

A few minutes after we boarded, Shai made an announcement into the microphone that we would be stopping by the market and we should pick up desserts for a party we would have later that night. There was a general tone of cheer after the announcement.

Ben was still upset about missing out on the Old City, but we were sitting together on the bus and planning our escape from our guided tour. We only had one more day of the Birthright trip. After that, we were both extending our stay. He was staying for another three days, and I was staying for another three months.

We plotted about the places we could see once we were autonomous again and let out into Tel-Aviv on our own. We continued to talk excitedly, even as we unloaded the bus and entered the market near our hotel.

"Okay guys, you have about half an hour before we need to leave here to get ready for Shabbat, so hurry," Shai announced letting us loose in Jerusalem.

I parted ways with Ben to cover more ground faster. As I walked down the old cobblestone street, I spotted a coffee shop. It is inevitable that I must stop and get coffee upon these sightings, even when running against a stopwatch. As I went to enter the shop Angelica spotted me.

"Hey, good idea," she said joining me and we entered together. We spent most of the thirty minutes of our free time talking about our experience at the wall as we sipped coffee at the counter. In the remaining minutes we dashed to get treats for our evening and quickly rejoined our group.

Upon arriving back at the hotel we were informed that dinner was ready and we should eat quickly and meet back in the lobby for an off-campus

Heavy military presence at the Western Wall. Jerusalem.

Shabbat ceremony. When we entered the dining hall, it was overflowing. I noticed Shai talking with someone in charge, who reluctantly made space for us in the already full dining room. It seemed that Shai had effectively coerced something from someone at each of our destinations that day. Whatever he lacked in other areas, he certainly made up for with his efficiency and adaptability. I guessed that he must have been one of the star employees of Taglit. We ate quickly, as instructed.

When we met downstairs, Shai introduced us to a rabbi and his family. We would be celebrating Shabbat with them that night.

"We are very happy to have you all come visit us this evening as we celebrate Shabbat together," he said charmingly as he pulled his family close.

We left at once and walked quickly back through the quiet streets of Jerusalem. Despite being one of our last days, our agenda was still packed full. I took long strides to keep up with the pace. I was already fatigued, and we still had a night of dessert sharing planned after this adventure.

After many blocks and turns we quietly entered into a garden ceremony that was already in progress. Large trees and shrubbery covered the outdoor space that was lit faintly with cool blue LED tea lights and lamps. It was as if a hundred fireflies were dancing in the cool air. I noticed the garden was partitioned into two sections; men and women.

The guys of our group moved past the women's section and over to the other side. A song was in progress as we joined the group. We were given a sort of program to follow, but it was written in Hebrew. The song transitioned into a prayer and back into a song. Each new tune had more energy and more ooos and ahhs than the last. All of the seats on the women's side were taken, so I moved past where the partition wall ended and found standing room in the back. I noticed that the men's side did not seem to have any chairs. No one was sitting. As the songs grew louder and more full of life, the men began to spring into dance, grabbing other men and swinging around. They chanted and laughed loudly as they urged our male group members to join them. On our side, most of the movement came from the dangling feet of seated, cross-legged women. The juxtaposition was annoying, so I made my way back toward the front and behind the partition. I found a seat on a fallen tree trunk, out of sight, and looked out into the blue night. Despite the segregation of gender, the religious context, and the general awkwardness of it all, it was still a beautiful garden full of people yelling about things they love at dusk. That's a lovely sight in almost any context.

As we walked back to the hotel, I wandered between conversations and got lost in my own thoughts. The day was marked by a gender divide. It was a topic that I had wondered about earlier in the trip, but was more present on this day than ever before. Shai had once told us that women and men are separate during religious ceremonies so that the men are not distracted by a woman. However, this does little to prevent a woman being distracted by a woman or a man by a man. He had no response to this question. I remembered the short conversation we had a few days earlier.

One of our female trip mates asked Shai genuinely, "What would a transgender person do in these situations?"

Shai looked confused and mumbled, "What is that?"

The gender binary does much to ostracize transgender people all over the world. Even "progressive" countries and cultures still have primitive comprehension of differently-gendered people. In January of 2015, a transgender Israeli woman visiting the Western Wall was denied access to the women's side by an Orthodox woman, acting as the "moral police," who said she was not a woman. She was then denied access to the men's side because she did not look like a man. She eventually left the holy place after being denied entry.

I recalled when the young woman who had asked Shai the question began to describe to him what transgender meant. He looked baffled and the conversation awkwardly died.

My thoughts were interrupted when we got back to the hotel. We ate desserts, drank wine, and played card games into the night. We only had one more day on the trip and I had become eager for it to end.

Chapter 13: Final Day ... Did someone say "Birthrate"?

We woke up slowly on our final day. I think it was the first morning I had the opportunity to sleep in since I had arrived. It was Shabbat again and that meant we would be doing a lot of activities in the hotel, or things within walking distance. Luckily, the Israel Museum was one of those sites.

I took the morning to write in my journal, something I had found no time to do while on this trip. Everyday had been so busy and full of noise that it was impossible to process my thoughts without interruption.

I finally made my way downstairs around 11:00 a.m. and joined my group for the walk to the museum. Shai, dressed mostly in white, led us out into the empty streets of Jerusalem. It was supposed to be a "walking tour" of the city, but it was mostly just a walk to the museum. Shai did not address us as a group until we reached the museum gates.

"Listen up everybody," he began, "You're going to have a museum tour guide take you from here," he announced.

There were mumbles of annoyance from some, including myself. Most of us were tired of being guided and had hoped we would have more autonomy in the museum. We were wrong, as usual.

Shai left us at the entrance and we were split into two smaller and more manageable groups. Ben and I got different assignments but pretended we didn't know that and went with the same tour guide.

In an attempt to see things that interested us, we stood close to the guide and suggested things she should show us. It worked, and we spent most of our time in the contemporary art wing. Unfortunately, it was a section our guide seemed to know very little about.

"This is a video called War of Independence," she said, motioning for us to take a seat in an empty room as a video of images looped in front of us.

Video from Israeli Independence Day footage was spliced with images of meat on a grill, fire, guns, and fireworks.

After several minutes passed she asked, "What do you see here?"

I answered, "Patriarchy."

She nodded subtly. No one else offered opinions. Ben smirked.

We spent over an hour wandering the contemporary art, where many of the artists' work was highly political. Our guide had minimal knowledge of the time periods or of political ideologies of the artists. After several failed attempts at sparking conversation, we were released back into the main foyer to wait for Shai to pick us up.

He appeared after a while and we walked back to the hotel, mostly in silence. When we entered the lobby we were instructed that we would have a conversation downstairs with the rabbi who had been our host the night before. We headed down to the bomb shelter classroom where he was already waiting.

"Hello again," he said as soon as we entered the room.

We took our seats without expectations. This lecture wasn't on our itinerary.

"I am happy that Shai allowed me to come talk with you all this afternoon. I really enjoyed having you join us last night for our Shabbat ceremony," he began. "Today I want to present you with a little dilemma," he said with a nefarious grin. "I teach in Jerusalem and I've found this topic to always provide a great place for debate," he said. "It's a simple dilemma in which you must choose a side," he explained.

We sat quietly, with little interest in his alluring setup. We had been guided and lectured across Israel and we were sitting in yet another lecture—this one unplanned—before another one in just a few hours.

"Okay, here it is," he said. "You and your friends go on a spelunking adventure. You are all in a cave when out of nowhere, BOOM!" he exclaimed. "An avalanche," he said, explaining his sound effects.

"Rocks have fallen down the mountain and closed in the mouth of the cave, all except one small hole which is filtering in light," he paused, letting us imagine the scene. "Filled with some relief that you are not completely buried in, you notice that the cave is filling quickly with water. It is already at your ankles and rising. Suddenly, your friend Bob goes running toward the light, he climbs the rocks frantically and tries to escape but he's too fat to fit through. He's pushed himself headfirst through the hole and is unable to move any further," he said excitedly. "Now, everyone is frantic, scared, and no one can get Bob out of the hole. The water keeps rising!" he yelled. "Then someone in your group announces that they have a stick of dynamite."

He paused making sure we got all the details.

"Okay, now here are your options. Use the dynamite to blow the wall of fallen rocks away, thus killing Bob, or, let the water rise and sacrifice yourselves for Bob's life."

He smiled as we began to think of the side we would choose. He instructed us to pick a side of the room based on our decision and then we would talk about the reasons we chose what we did.

Most of our group went to the side that would kill Bob. A few kind souls went to the side of sacrifice. I remained in my chair, which was on no particular side. Brian, who sat beside me, also did not move.

"Okay," the rabbi said watching us choose sides. "Let's hear from someone on each side," he said.

He called on one of our most masculine group members to present his reason for choosing to kill Bob.

"The fat dude shouldn't have got stuck in the hole. We gotta kill him!" he shouted.

His side roared in agreement. All of the men in our group, except Brian, were on that side.

"Okay, what about from the side that would sacrifice themselves?" he asked choosing someone to speak from that side.

"Killing him to save our lives is still murder," one of the more soft-spoken girls answered.

"Okay, so let's hear about you two in the middle here," he said pointing at Brian.

Brian did not look comfortable or prepared to share his opinion and was quiet after he was called upon.

"Perhaps you are suggesting there is another way?" the rabbi asked without waiting for Brian to speak.

Brian nodded in approval.

"Perhaps you can ask Bob what he would like to do?" he offered as Brian's opinion. "If Bob has to make the decision then it won't be on you to decide, right?" He asked slyly.

"Okay, so who would choose this option?" He asked the group.

A few people from each side now joined the space near Brian and myself.

This fictional debate went on for far too long, with the room being split into endless categories of what-ifs. It was the only group conversation that escalated to extreme emotional heights. I was disgusted by some of the opinions as each new twist was introduced.

"What if he has discovered the cure for cancer? What if he's a psychopath and got stuck in the hole on purpose? What if he's fat because he's depressed?" The rabbi offered up more and more twists until the tension was unbearable.

Alliances formed on the topic as three or four strong opinions were being heard. Most of the group was quiet and uncomfortable. I was one of the most verbal and annoyed. At first, I was annoyed by the irrelevance of the topic and how opinionated everyone was about the fictitious situation, but then, I felt the need to voice an opinion against the insincere in the room. I voiced strong opposition to killing Bob and spoke up mostly because no women were, and a group of muscle heads was rallying toward murder. As tempers flared around the topic, I thought of Palestine, yet again. Here we were, in the country that had set fire to the proverbial dynamite in attempt to secure "freedom" and we were arguing about a fictional spelunking adventure. It was obvious that the rabbi intended this exercise to be a metaphor for Palestine and I knew the opinions around Bob presented by most of my trip mates here would likely mirror opinions around Palestinians.

Eventually, after an uproarious conversation, the rabbi asked us to take a seat and allow him to wrap up. We sat, darting eyes at our new ideological enemies.

"It's complicated," he began. "It's a hard question to answer and there are always new ways to look for a solution. But when things keep changing, it's hard to pick a side," he said. "I want you to think about this when you go back to the US and reflect on the Middle East and Israel," he finished.

There was a small applause and Shai released us quickly so we could have some free time before our next lecture.

I was annoyed and nearly speechless by both the opinions of some of my trip mates and that in response to the political situation of the Middle East we were offered only this:

"It's Complicated."

What's complicated? I asked myself as we left the classroom.

"Hey," Brian said, getting my attention.

"Hey," I returned as I fell into step with him.

"You okay?" he asked, chuckling a little bit.

"Oh, I doubt it," I said with a smirk. "I am very ready to be out of this group." I responded.

Over the past nine days, I had speculated and quietly judged some of my trip mates that had demonstrated different levels of insincerity. This was the first time I had said anything aloud about it. As we walked upstairs and into the lobby, the guy with whom I had been most adversarial with was standing at the mouth of the staircase. In line with awkwardness, we locked eyes.

"Hey, you're like, the best person ever. I admire you," he said as we stood facing each other.

"Oh?" I asked sarcastically.

"Yeah, you're like Gandhi," he said smiling. "For real."

"I'm like Gandhi cause I wouldn't automatically kill a man to save my life?" I asked him.

He nodded and smiled and we parted ways.

Ben, Brian, and I walked outside and stood with the smokers. The afternoon air was warm. I felt my skin defrosting from the classroom goose bumps chill.

"Poor Bob," Ben said scoffing and blowing smoke from his cigarette. "I'm glad you stood up for him," he said smiling at me.

"I wasn't trying to seem heroic. It's just that, one, there's never room for any of the girls on our trip to speak and I've watched plenty of them think about saying something while waiting far too patiently for one of the five outspoken men on our trip to finish up." I took a breath, "Two, the energy of the group that wanted Bob's head was driven by adrenaline and bullshit,"

I said smirking and holding up a third finger. “And three, someone has to stand up to meatheads.” I said laughing.

“Truthfully,” I began when Ben’s laughter died down, “I wish I hadn’t let myself be so affected by this lecture.” I paused and sighed, “But since we will never have a political conversation about Palestine or any real issues while we’re here, I had to speak up, at least for the women who didn’t have a voice on this trip.”

Ben gave me an empathetic sideways smile.

“Yeah, this trip was designed with one side in mind,” he said, “but at least we get to stay afterward and have a real experience.” He reminded me.

The three of us decided to go upstairs and plan where we would go in Israel after we were released. Brian, who was also extending his trip, was set on coming back to Jerusalem to visit the Old City. Ben only had a few more days so he resigned to spend it all in Tel-Aviv. I had months of time to spare and no definite plans. We spent our free time all piled near the window in my hotel room, where we could steal Wi-Fi from a neighboring building. The hotel we were staying at charged ten dollars per half hour for access to their Wi-Fi.

I had found a place for Ben and I to stay for two nights in Tel Aviv. We would be couch surfing with a young man just out of the military who had a nice place in the city’s center. He was very excited to have us and we were very excited to fraternize with a culture we had only seen through the Birthright lens.

My roommates joined us halfway through our Internet pirate party and poured us cups of wine. We sat around making jokes and falling into deliriousness. About fifteen minutes after the time we were supposed to be downstairs for our next lecture, Ben shot up.

“Shit! We’re late!” he exclaimed, looking at his watch.

We burst into laughter and scurried toward the door with our cups of wine still in our hands.

We hustled down the six flights of stairs into the basement. Our lecture had already started in the main classroom downstairs. We scattered out among the empty chairs we could find. Shai looked at our late entrance with annoyance.

As I took a seat, I noticed the room was full of people I didn’t recognize. At least two other Birthright groups must have been here for this lecture as well. I sipped my wine, shook my head, and sighed out of irritation. There was no way, with this many people, that there would be a conversation. There were nearly one hundred of us in a room for a lecture titled, "The Situation Today in Israel," and it was being facilitated by one of the most prominent Israel Advocacy speakers, Neil Lazarus. All of these factors meant one thing to me: more propaganda and no way around it.

I drank more wine as a handout was passed around. The visual aid was a big sub sandwich, with each part of it representing different countries in the Middle East.

"You can see in your handouts that I've used a sandwich to explain what's going on in the Middle East," Mr. Lazarus began in an English accent. "I like to use food in examples because I am fat," he said chuckling.

There was a burst of laughter from the audience. He went on for a bit about his weight, making several jokes at his own expense. Everyone was laughing. I chuckled as I looked at the handout and sipped more wine.

For the next hour, he spoke uninterrupted, during which he victimized Israel and demonized the surrounding nations. Cleverly, he left Palestine out of his lecture. I ran out of wine far too early into the presentation. As he went on, he made more jokes, made more and more people laugh, all the while, convincing everyone that Israel was small, vulnerable to attack at any moment, and that the nation was in a sort of constant danger.

"Now why do you think we are in a bomb shelter during this lecture?" he asked nefariously.

He used comedic relief between his serious statements to soften the blow.

"It's complicated," he uttered. "I put that on my Facebook and my wife was very upset," he joked.

There it was again. *It's complicated.*

Everyone laughed again. For most in the room, he was a funny guy. He was a great public speaker, he was able to keep attention and use humor. However, I found his use of comedy to be his scariest trait. He was the Patch Adams of Israel Advocacy, making the pill of an apartheid state easier to swallow. I could not laugh.

He retrieved his handouts and took only a few questions at the end of his lecture, making sure to evade the one brave soul who asked about a two-state solution.

"I believe the answer to peace is with the leaders," he answered and quickly took another question. I scoffed at his answer and looked over at Ben, who looked eager to leave.

"I want to thank you all for listening to me this afternoon," he said in closing. "I know it's your last day of Birthrate and you're ready to get out of here," he chuckled.

I looked at him with my jaw agape.

"It's not a secret, right?" He said laughing. "I think it used to be more hush hush, but we all know this trip is really about *birthrate*, right?" He joked unforgivingly. "Anyway you kids, you get out there and enjoy your last day. Rumor has it if you get hitched to someone on this trip you can get a free honeymoon in Israel," he joked again looking around the room for contention among any Birthright organizers.

There was a nervous laughter from the audience and then an awkward silence. I was stunned to hear someone speak so honestly about what had seemed like a hidden agenda.

At the door, he handed out his business card and suggested we download the Neil Lazarus App for our smart phones. He was by far the most offensive speaker we had witnessed, and the most charming.

"Whoa," Ben said as we burst through the door of my hotel room. "That guy was a piece of work," he said, sitting on the edge of the bed.

Brian and the girls poured more wine and we all sat around the room.

"He lectures to over thirty thousand people a year," I said, reading the fact from his website.

"It also says he's been called "Mr. Israel Advocacy" by *The Times of Israel*, Ben said reading over my shoulder.

"He's bringing home the pork-free bacon," Brian joked.

We laughed as I tossed his card into a pile of other propaganda I had collected on the trip. I sat near the window and responded to an email making arrangements with our couchsurfer host for the next day.

After what seemed like only a few minutes, we were running down for dinner and then back down to the bomb shelter for Havdalah, an end of Shabbat ceremony, and some final words from Shai.

The sun was setting as we made our way from the cafeteria to the classroom downstairs. When we entered the classroom, the rabbi from earlier was standing at the front of the room.

"Oh no, not again," I whispered to no one in particular as I took a seat.

"It's good to see you all again," he said once we were settled. "Shai asked me to lead you in Havdalah this evening." He explained.

We all stood in a circle, lit a candle, and passed around a bouquet of smelling herbs, meant to reawaken your spirit after a day of rest. Ironically, we hadn't rested since we arrived, but I still enjoyed the smell.

The lights were turned back on when we were done with the call and response prayer that ends Shabbat. We all took our seats again.

"I would like to share a story with you," the rabbi said. "It's a story I tell my children every night at bedtime."

I shook my head and stared wide eyed in pre-emptive boredom. He began to tell a story of a man who needed money and who leaves home to find work, followed by something about getting paid in chicken fat, and then there was a moral. All of it was lost on me, and from the looks on faces around the room, I would say he confused everyone, including Shai.

He thanked us again and finally departed. Shai shut the door behind him and stood in front of us. He took a moment before speaking.

"So, Amy, Sara, and I would like to take a few minutes to thank you for such a wonderful trip," he began with emotion in his voice. "I have been doing this for a very long time, and you have been one of the best and most responsible groups I've ever had," he admitted.

I could not believe we were the responsible ones, but, the typical age group for Birthright tours is between eighteen and twenty years old, so I suppose he meant we were a more mature group.

He became a little flustered and motioned for Sara and Amy to talk. Each girl reflected on her experience with our group, referenced inside jokes, and thanked us for a great experience. Shai gained his composure and thanked us again.

"It's early, so I hope you find time to say goodbye to your new friends tonight. You only have one more thing to do for me," he said, pausing. "Please be in the lobby by 6:00 a.m. so we can be in Tel Aviv in time for your flight home."

Shai smiled. He knew it was customary for everyone to stay up late on their last night in Israel, and he let us have a large portion of the evening free. He dismissed us, and many people went up to say goodbye to him and thank him personally for such a great trip. I stood with Ben and Brian as we tried to dissect what that fairy tale meant.

"Hey, party in room 601," one of the muscle-heads said leaning into our conversation. "The soldiers are gonna be there," he said with dirty smirk.

"Oh, the cool kids invited us to party," Brian joked.

I had thought we would never see the soldiers again, but I overheard that each one was expected to return. Each room had at least three people in it and negotiations were in place for which rooms would be vacant for last-night hook-ups.

We walked upstairs and opened our last bottle of wine, poured ourselves glasses, and headed down to the lobby. A few of us gathered on couches and sat talking for a bit. After a few minutes, three giggling girls swept through the lobby, stopping off at our gathering.

"The stores are opened up again since Shabbat is over," they whispered. "We're gonna get some beer. Do you want anything?" they asked.

"I'll just go with you," I said, curious to see if I could find any snacks.

"I'll join you," Ben announced, and we all headed toward the store.

It was attached to the hotel but on a side I had never seen. A neon light that read, "24/6" was illuminated in the window. I chuckled at the sight and pointed it out to Ben.

While we were browsing the cookie catalog, a group of four more Birthright attendees pushed through the doors and headed toward the beer and wine. Ben and I bought cookies and headed back to the hotel.

"It's gonna get rowdy tonight," Ben joked.

We joined the smoking circle outside and ate cookies. Our guard, who lives in Jerusalem, had gone home to get his guitar and another guy on our trip was strumming it. He began to sing and everyone fell silent to the obligatory awkward listening that is customary under these circumstances.

He sang, obstructing the path to the hotel lobby. Eventually, he was interrupted when the soldiers from our mifgash showed up and began to make their way inside. I followed them in and noticed that the group we had abandoned on the couches had left.

"Hey, I heard there's some folks hanging out in Michael's room upstairs, I think it's 604," Ben said, joining me again.

"Okay," I returned. "But let's stop off and get more wine," I said looking at my empty cup.

He nodded in approval and we headed upstairs. We spent many hours bouncing around from rooms with parties to the lobby and the smoking circle outside. Later in the night, close to midnight, we stood outside conversing with the inebriated smokers and guitar strummers. A deep philosophical conversation was spinning its wheels in the inebriated minds of its speakers. Suddenly, we all fell quiet. One of the male soldiers was whisking away one our female trip mates toward his car. We stared in silence until they were out of earshot.

"Oh boy," I exclaimed as we fell into laughter. "Isn't she engaged?" I asked.

Ben nodded sadly.

A few minutes later the bellhop came outside to tell us that they would lock the doors in half an hour. We looked at each other and then toward the parking lot.

"Half an hour is enough time," somebody said.

"Maybe we should go find his car?" another voice suggested.

"Nah, they'll be fine." I answered.

We left the butt-filled ashtrays with the guitar and headed inside. I found the cool-kids party upstairs. Most of the soldiers were there. The beds had been turned into couches, and Israeli music videos were playing loudly on the television. I attempted to mingle, but then quickly retreated back to my floor. When I got off the elevator I found Ben, Brian, Angelica, and Liora and Abe, the same group I had come out to on the shores of Tel Aviv just a few days earlier.

"Thank God," I exclaimed and joined them on the couches. I plopped down heavily and checked the clock. It was almost 2:00 a.m.

"Wanna play cards?" Angelica asked, already dealing me in.

A few games in, we heard the elevator door open. Another male soldier and a girl from our group darted by our couches.

She turned back and whispered, "Don't tell anyone you saw me."

They ran off through the halls. Some minutes after that, her good friend came looking for her. We denied we had seen anyone and continued playing cards.

Somewhere after 3:00 a.m. we decided to turn in for a few hours before we had to leave for the airport.

* * *

The bus ride to Tel Aviv was mostly quiet. I stared nervously out of the same window seat I had occupied during the entire trip. There is always a certain excited uneasiness that overcomes me before I venture out onto trips alone. I was ready to be out of the chokehold of the Birthright agenda and to explore Israel on my own terms. I was eager to ask questions that I did not feel I could before. Privately, I was nervous about it all, too.

Forty-five minutes after we boarded the bus, we were unloading at Ben Gurion International Airport in Tel Aviv. I watched my sleepy trip mates gather their luggage for the last time. Nearly everyone on the trip was headed home with what is often referred to as "an experience of a lifetime!" I predicted many from our group would repeat this line to their friends and family for years after they returned home.

Ben, Brian, and I were obliged to join our group all the way to the ticket counter before we could be released. I stood holding the plastic handle of my cheap and beaten suitcase as we said our casual goodbyes. Amy and Sara took the rest of the group that was headed home to the ticket counter to begin checking in.

"Have fun you guys," Amy said smiling.

The three of us gathered our belongings as they all walked away. We turned toward the doors we had just entered. It was the first time I felt autonomous in ten days. I slipped my sunglasses over my eyes and kicked my suitcase onto its back wheels.

"Where do we go?" Ben asked.

I shrugged and headed toward the exit.

ON OUR OWN AUTHORITY! PUBLISHING

Founded in 2012, On Our Own Authority! is a volunteer-run autonomous research press based in Atlanta, Georgia. We specialize in anarchist and radical literature, publishing intellectual history, social movement history, and studies of global political thought that emphasize themes of anti-colonialism, direct democracy, and workers' self-management.

www.oooabooks.org

Other titles now available:

Faith Beauchemin,
How Queer!: Personal narratives from bisexual, pansexual, polysexual, sexually fluid and other non-monosexual persepctives.

Lenni Brenner,
Zionism in the Age of the Dictators

Lenni Brenner and Mathew Quest,
Black Liberation and Palestine Solidarity

Joseph Edwards,
Workers' Self-Management in the Caribbean

Christian Hogsbjerg,
Chris Braithwaite: Mariner, Renegade and Castaway

Sen Katayama,
The Labor Movement in Japan

Kimathi Mohammed,
Organization and Spontaneity

Ida B. Wells,
Lynch Law in Georgia & Other Writings